Free Speech

Key Concepts in Political Theory series

Free Speech

Matteo Bonotti
Jonathan Seglow

polity

The right of Matteo Bonotti and Jonathan Seglow to be identified as Author of this Work has been asserted in accordance with the UK Copyright, Designs and Patents Act 1988.

First published in 2021 by Polity Press

Polity Press
65 Bridge Street
Cambridge CB2 1UR, UK

Polity Press
101 Station Landing
Suite 300
Medford, MA 02155, USA

ISBN-13: 978-1-5095-2644-4
ISBN-13: 978-1-5095-2645-1 (pb)

A catalogue record for this book is available from the British Library.

Library of Congress Cataloging-in-Publication Data
Names: Bonotti, Matteo, author. | Seglow, Jonathan, 1968- author.
Title: Free speech / Matteo Bonotti, Jonathan Seglow.
Description: Cambridge, UK ; Medford, MA : Polity, 2021. | Series: Key concepts in political theory | Includes bibliographical references and index. | Summary: "A compact guide to the major debates about what restrictions, if any, should be placed on free expression"-- Provided by publisher.
Identifiers: LCCN 2020048713 (print) | LCCN 2020048714 (ebook) | ISBN 9781509526444 (hardback) | ISBN 9781509526451 (paperback) | ISBN 9781509526482 (epub)
Subjects: LCSH: Freedom of speech--United States.
Classification: LCC JC591 .B683 2021 (print) | LCC JC591 (ebook) | DDC 323.44/30973--dc23
LC record available at https://lccn.loc.gov/2020048713
LC ebook record available at https://lccn.loc.gov/2020048714

Typeset in 10.5 on 12pt Sabon
by Fakenham Prepress Solutions, Fakenham, Norfolk NR21 8NL
Printed and bound in Great Britain by Short Run Press

For further information on Polity, visit our website:
politybooks.com

Contents

Introduction

The 2016 Brexit referendum in the United Kingdom, Donald Trump's election as president of the United States and re-election campaign in 2020, the rise of right-wing populism in Europe and further afield, the current wave of Islamophobia and anti-Semitism, and the hate speech targeting people of Chinese origin during the COVID-19 pandemic have brought freedom of speech to the forefront of public and academic debate, together with the question of whether hateful expression ought to be regulated. The tension between freedom of speech and offensiveness also continues to elicit controversy, as shown for example by the 2006 *Jyllands-Posten* Muhammad cartoons controversy and, more recently, by the attacks on *Charlie Hebdo*'s offices in Paris in 2015 and 2020. The growing availability of Internet pornography has reignited long-standing debates between liberal and feminist thinkers concerning the permissibility of censorship and the tension between individual freedom and harm to women. Last but not least, recent phenomena such as fake news, trans wars and race culture wars have spurred new controversies regarding whether, when and how online speech should be regulated.

For example, in June 2020 Joanne K. Rowling, the author of *Harry Potter*, posted the following tweet in response to a headline about 'people who menstruate': '"People who menstruate". I'm sure there used to be a word for those people. Someone help me out. Wumben? Wimpund? Woomud?'.[1] Soon Rowling became the target of countless tweets accusing her of transphobia.[2] In another example, in September 2020 US President Donald Trump attacked the Black Lives Matter movement and stated that '[l]eft-wing mobs have torn down statues of our founders, desecrated our memorials and carried out a campaign of violence and anarchy … Whether it is the mob on the street, or the cancel culture in the boardroom, the goal is the same: to silence dissent, to scare you out of speaking the truth and to bully Americans into abandoning their values.'[3] The contentiousness of the debates that followed these and similar incidents renders the theoretical analysis of freedom of speech, and of its permissible limits, both necessary and urgent.

Asking why exactly free speech should be protected is not a redundant task. Free speech informs the political world in which we live. Most liberal democracies have the right to free speech enshrined in their constitutions and bills of rights – the US First Amendment is the most famous example. Even many non-democratic states pay lip service to free speech, though they may not always respect it in practice. The UN Declaration of Human Rights gives a prominent place to free speech, as does the European Convention on Human Rights, along with other declarations and charters. But all these documents are, essentially, the expression of our shared attachment to the value of free speech among other basic liberties; they do not tell us *why* free speech is among their clauses or articles and *why* those who drafted constitutions and the like thought it important to include free speech in the first place. After all, constitutions can get it wrong, or at least contain principles that are highly contested. It is controversial, for example, whether Americans really have a human, as opposed to a constitutional, right to carry a weapon, and until 2018 it was unconstitutional in Ireland for women to seek an abortion.

That people do not often reflect on these questions is also evident from our everyday experience. For example, when we ask students, during lectures or seminars, whether and why hate speech laws or other forms of censorship are wrong, a response we often receive is: 'Of course these are wrong, they violate free speech!' But when pressed to explain why there should be free speech in the first instance, students often find it harder to articulate good arguments in support of it; they often seem to assume that the value of free speech is somehow self-evident. This assumption risks transforming our commitment to free speech into an ideological dogma and leaves little room for justifying the regulation of certain kinds of speech, even when we find them intuitively abhorrent.

We have an interest in knowing why free speech is significant both because we would benefit from articulating the common intuition that it is and because free speech may be limited by laws and regulations – or, less formally, by the power of social sanction (as when someone fears the stigma of expressing an unpopular view); and, if these limits come up against the value of free speech, we want to know what that value is. Perhaps free speech is not actually valuable in some circumstances, where it is limited – hate speech may be one example – but, again, establishing this requires an understanding of what its value is in the first place.

In exploring this question, it is worth noting in the first place that speech may actually be limited in all sorts of ways that are not at all controversial. Bribery, perjury, harassment, discrimination, plagiarism, copyright violations, selling state secrets, price fixing, insider trading, defamation and threatening somebody with a weapon are illegal in most jurisdictions, but, because we are communicative creatures, they all involve speech in some way. So why should we not be free to engage in them? The basic answer is that these are all forms of wrongful *conduct*, not just speech. But the distinction between speech and conduct is far from simple. After all, if someone offers you a job, warns you that there is traffic ahead, or says that she wants to divorce you, she is also acting in various ways, not simply speaking, even though these are all perfectly legitimate instances of free speech. By contrast, wrongful conduct invades people's autonomy, violates their rights, puts them at risk, arbitrarily treats some worse than others, and so on; and in such instances speech is inextricably bound up with these harms. As we will see in cases where free speech is controversial, those who argue for limits argue precisely along these lines: they point out that speech involves some sort of harm or injustice, for example that hate speech invades autonomy or that pornography is an act of subordinating women.

'Speech' in the phrase 'free speech' is a term of art and does not actually refer to *all* speech. For one thing, beyond the public square and people's homes, all institutions police free speech norms that enable them to achieve their purposes. Thus a political party can expel a member who failed to honour its basic ideological commitments; a company can reprimand an employee who helped the competition; or a church can refuse to recognise a worshipper who rejected its central religious tenets. (This aspect will become especially relevant when we discuss free speech in universities in Chapter 6.)

In general, the kind of speech that free speech advocates regard as most important to protect is that of people who express themselves on moral, political, cultural, religious, historical, literary, scientific and similarly weighty issues, especially within a public or an associational setting – as opposed to speech among friends, family and other intimates that states are not generally interested in regulating (though there are exceptions). The former is often called 'high-value' speech. By contrast, 'low-value' speech is public or associational speech that has implications for people in that it can affect their interests in ways that might be normatively troubling. Examples of this kind of speech are libel, slander and defamation; invasion of privacy; commercial advertising; abusive, insulting and offensive speech; hate speech; and pornography. But, although the high-value–low-value distinction is often invoked in free speech debates and we will employ it ourselves later on, it is important to remember that this is not a stable distinction either. One person's serious artistic expression may be another person's pornography, for example.

In this book we elaborate on these sorts of considerations in order to address the complex dimensions of free speech. In Chapter 1 we examine the three 'classic' theories of free speech, grounded in the values of truth, autonomy and democracy. We identify different strands within each theory, consider some of the main criticisms that have been raised against each one of them and comment on their relationship to one another. This three-part framework informs our analysis throughout the subsequent chapters by providing some normative guidelines for assessing when the regulation of free speech may be morally permissible, or even obligatory.

Chapter 2 examines the much debated topic of hate speech. As well as asking what hate speech is, we consider various contexts in which this kind of speech manifests itself and illustrate some different ways in which it is regulated in different jurisdictions. We discuss what implications the truth, autonomy and democracy arguments have for hate speech, then go on to consider further arguments in favour of hate speech regulation. We also examine the complex issues surrounding the design of laws that restrict hate speech and we consider non-regulatory responses to such laws, including counterspeech.

In Chapter 3 we focus on Holocaust denial as an exemplary case of speech whose limitations are often subject to debate. While often considered a form of hate speech, Holocaust denial presents distinctive challenges. Given the central role that epistemic historical claims play in it, we consider in some detail the implications of the truth argument for its regulation. Yet Holocaust denial also raises important questions regarding individual autonomy and democracy. We explore the former especially in relation to educational settings and online platforms, and the latter by considering the role of Holocaust denial within broader political worldviews.

Chapter 4 examines offensive speech. Although it is sometimes conflated with hate speech, more often than not offensive speech is considered a much less harmful kind of speech. But what, if anything, is wrong with it? After sketching a brief account of the origins of offence in blasphemy law, we address this question by identifying moral, conventional and raw offence and by analysing the first two categories in relation to the truth, autonomy and democracy arguments for free speech. We conclude by discussing Joel Feinberg's (1985) influential defence of regulating offensive speech and point to some problems with it.

In Chapter 5 we consider the question of whether and why pornography, as a mode of speech, should be regulated. After briefly examining the view that pornography might possess some social value, we consider different types of harms that pornography is often accused of inflicting on women. These include harms to women involved in the pornography industry; the sexual violence or discrimination encouraged by the consumption of pornographic materials; and the view that pornography harms women in society more generally, by inherently subordinating or silencing them. We show why, though pornography might in principle advance the values of autonomy and democracy, it is more often likely to undermine them.

Chapter 6 tackles three pressing issues at the forefront of contemporary public debate on contemporary free speech. The first concerns the policy of no-platforming, adopted by university students in the United States, the United Kingdom and elsewhere. This is a policy of denying controversial speakers external to the university a platform to speak from in that university – which makes it another case of policing free speech norms. We consider the complex relationship between academic debate and free speech, and examine whether there is a case for no-platforming on the basis of the values that universities exist to promote. The other two issues examined in the chapter are, both, related to free speech in online environments. One is fake news: 'the deliberate presentation of (typically) false or misleading claims as news, where the claims are misleading *by design*' (Gelfert 2018, pp. 85–6). The other is online public shaming: the use of social sanctions through speech in order to criticise those who have allegedly done or said something wrong (another example of speech as conduct). We examine recent work in political theory that has begun to address fake news and online public shaming and investigate ways in which the three arguments for free speech can help us to make sense of them.

We conclude with some brief reflections on free speech and liberalism's self-understanding.

In a short book like this one we have had to leave out much material that is interesting and relevant to the debate on free speech. Rather than examine in detail every new development that affects the frontiers of free speech – children's unfiltered online access, cyberbullying, the heated debate between some feminists and the trans community, the replacement of mainstream media by personalised social media in the delivery of news and current affairs, for instance

– we have opted for explaining long-standing debates about the nature, value and limits of speech (though in Chapter 6 and elsewhere we say a little about some new controversies, too). In this way we can at least understand how established theories of free speech might address such developments. We hope to show why and how free speech matters – but also why other values sometimes matter more.

We are grateful to George Owers and three anonymous reviewers for their constructive and insightful feedback on earlier drafts of this book. We would also like to thank Julia Davies and Manuela Tecusan for all their support and advice throughout the production process.

1
Theories of Free Speech

Introduction

There are plenty of potential justifications for free speech – explanations of why it is so valuable and important; and they tend to have a liberal flavour. One might argue that societies that respect their citizens' free speech, especially on political and related matters, are more stable, more peaceful and more tolerant than societies that do not; or, relatedly, that free speech functions as a kind of safety valve, enabling citizens to express grievances without resorting to disorder or violence. Those grievances might take the form of low-value hate speech. Another justification is that many people value diversity and pluralism in political, artistic, religious, cultural and academic matters and free speech will enable expression of these values much better than would the state enforcement of an orthodoxy.

Freedom of speech can also be defended along the lines of a characteristically liberal scepticism towards government power. Given that legislators and public officials are prone to limiting individuals' liberties for arbitrary or unjustifiable reasons, it is sensible to require them by law to protect free speech. As Frederick Schauer writes,

> Freedom of speech is based in large part on a distrust of the ability of government to make the necessary distinctions

[between speech that may be regulated], a distrust of governmental determinations of truth and falsity, an appreciation of the fallibility of political leaders, and a somewhat deeper distrust of government power in a more general sense. (Schauer 1982, p. 86)

It is no accident that all these are, broadly speaking, liberal arguments. Free speech is a liberal principle, indeed one of *the* liberal principles. This does not mean that other political perspectives cannot support free speech; socialist and conservative parties in democratic states generally and speech that may not support it too, for example. Nor does it mean that other philosophical and political views have nothing to offer the debate over free speech. In Chapter 5, when we look at pornography, for example, we will consider feminist, conservative, communitarian and virtue ethics arguments against pornography that stand opposed to liberal permissiveness. There are also recent efforts to outline a Marxist defence of free speech (Heinze 2018a, 2018b). But to claim that free speech is a liberal value is simply to draw attention to individual liberty, which is conceptually at its heart. This is true even if, as we will explore below, free speech is a matter of dialogue or democracy: it is speech between persons who are individually free to express and communicate their views. For this reason, apart from the exceptions noted, we shall not say very much about non-liberal approaches to free speech in this book.

We will focus instead on the three most prominent defences of free speech in the extensive literature on the topic. These theories are based on the values of truth, autonomy and democracy; and, as we will see, they are really families of views, since there are divisions within them. These three theories will help us to organise the discussion in the entire book, since they often have divergent – though sometimes overlapping – implications for deciding when speech may or should be limited.

In presenting these theories, we need to bear in mind two sets of distinctions. One is between claiming that free speech is valuable on the grounds that it is an essential means to achieve some further good, such as the good of diversity, or to avoid some harm, for example the harm of violent disorder, and claiming that free speech is inherently valuable independently of its consequences, as part of some larger moral or political ideal, for example the ideal that the value of personal autonomy should include the freedom to express oneself. The former type of claim is called consequentialist; the latter, deontological. The distinction between consequentialism and deontology is much discussed in moral philosophy and political theory, and free speech is almost certainly valuable for both sets of reasons (Greenawalt 1989). The other distinction we need to make is between our various interests: our interests qua speakers of all kinds; our interests qua audience of the speech of others – in other words our interests qua listeners, readers and viewers; and our interests qua bystanders involuntarily affected by the speech of others (see Scanlon 1979). Bystanders' interests become most relevant when we look at the harms produced by speech; but both speaker- and audience-based interests are especially relevant to the explanation of the value of speech, as we will now see.

Free speech and truth

The best known defence of freedom of speech in political thought is contained in John Stuart Mill's essay *On Liberty* (Mill 2006). Although this work was first published in 1859, Mill's argument for free speech remains a touchstone of contemporary debate, as does his stirring defence of liberty more generally. Mill's general project in *On Liberty* was to defend the 'harm principle', according to which individuals should be free to do as they wish, unless they harm others; only if they do is there ever a case for legal interference with individual liberty. Mill's argument is directed against social tyranny; his fear was that popular opinion, allied with the state, could be mobilised to limit the freedom of individuals whose lifestyles are judged foolish, ignoble, strange or avant-garde, since all these challenge majority norms. By contrast, Mill urges us to realise our individuality and to develop a character that is strong, independent-minded, authentic, confident in its convictions, free from the tyranny of the majority, and ready to engage in experiments on ways of living. All this is consistent with, indeed requires, vigorous debate with others.

Mill develops a specific argument for free speech in chapter 2 of *On Liberty*. It is noteworthy that he does *not* set out his argument by employing the concept of harm, in other words by arguing that speech is harmless to others. His interest is instead in the special value of speech, which goes above that of ordinary liberty. This special value consists in the fact that speech is necessary for discovering the truth; and, in Mill's view, knowing the truth is a source of happiness and well-being for both individuals and societies. Mill's argument for free speech is therefore a consequentialist one; according to him, '[t]he truth of an opinion is part of its utility' (Mill 2006, p. 29). This statement is best understood by considering Mill's defence of liberty and free speech in his other famous work, *Utilitarianism*, produced a few years later, in 1863 (Mill 1998): there Mill argues that individuals' actions, as well as the laws and policies of states, should be guided by the principle of maximising people's happiness or utility.

Although Mill talks a lot about truth in chapter 2 of *On Liberty*, his argument needs to be understood in an appropriate way. Truth makes sense in the natural sciences, but what about politics, history, economics, morality, ethics, literature, art and religion? Some people think that there are just different subjective views in these areas and that no one position is objectively true (we may call this 'Truth' with a capital T). Yet in all these domains there is ceaseless and often heated discussion and argument, as people advance their ideas and comment on the opinions of others. The views that survive this process are those that can be best defended *through the use of speech*; they are the most cogent, persuasive, convincing or justifiable ones, even if they are not true in the same way in which '2 + 2 = 4' is true. Conversely, views and opinions that do not convince or persuade others will tend to die away; they will have fewer (if any) adherents. The 'marketplace of ideas' is a metaphor often used in connection with Mill's argument for free speech, even if that precise phrase was first used by the US Supreme Court in *Abrams v United States* (1919), not by Mill. Just as competitively priced goods attract buyers in the economic market, driving out more expensive goods that are less appealing, so cogent and well-founded views will tend to win out over weaker ones in the realm of competing ideas.

But what is really important for Mill is the *process* of discovery of more well-founded views. As independent-minded individuals employing our reasoning capacities together, we discuss and deliberate about what is most significant, persuasive, justifiable and so on in various fields. This is what serves our happiness as progressive beings – a happiness of a higher kind. In principle one could imagine an omniscient dictatorship, which used censorship and indoctrination to ensure that citizens hold only true or valid opinions and did so even as it curtailed free speech (Ten 1980). But such a 'dictatorship of truth' would possess no value for Mill, because in his eyes utility ultimately resides in people's opportunity to employ their deliberative capacities. Robbed of this opportunity, citizens would not enjoy the practice of gradually arriving at more defensible views (cf. Brink 2008).

Three specific arguments for free speech, all based on the discovery of truth, can be found in the pages of Mill's long defence in *On Liberty*. First, he argues, free speech should be protected because otherwise some cogent or well-founded views would be silenced. As no one knows for sure which views those are, people who restrict the speech of others because they wrongly assume their own infallibility risk depriving themselves and others of the knowledge of silenced yet true opinions. This is often referred to as the *infallibility* argument. Among the many examples with which Mill illustrates it, that of Galileo Galilei (1564–1642) stands out as especially powerful. An early defender of heliocentrism, Galilei was forced by the Catholic Church to recant his views, which were considered heretical. This act of censorship, grounded in the Church's assumption that it infallibly 'knew' that the sun revolves around the earth, delayed people's appreciation of the scientific truth. More importantly, it deprived them of the utility that results from genuine knowledge of the universe and from the evaluation of that knowledge through their critical powers. Without free speech, the truth may take longer to emerge – if not fail to do so altogether.

Of course, suppressing free speech may on occasion silence opinions that are clearly false and not really worth hearing. These might include what we nowadays call 'fake news'. Mill maintains, however, that false opinions, too, play an important role in the marketplace of ideas. This is his second argument, known as the *dead dogma* argument. By challenging true opinions, false ones help those who know the truth to hold their views in a critical fashion rather than as unexamined ideas or prejudices whose grounds have been forgotten. When well-founded opinions are challenged by false ones, we are offered an opportunity to understand our own views better, as we are compelled to respond to misguided criticisms and flawed claims. If someone wrongly told us that 'all immigrants are criminals', for example, we could look at the data on crime, consider our views on the causes of crime, and come up with arguments to defeat our interlocutor, thereby employing our deliberative powers. As a result, well-founded views such as that criminals come from all walks of life and that most immigrants are not criminals would become more meaningful and lively in our minds.

Third, Mill argues that the most defensible position on many subjects is frequently not captured by any single view but is instead shared among different ones. Each view is therefore partially correct, and hence it is important to allow as many opinions as possible to circulate in order for the full truth to emerge (Mill 2006, p. 55). Political parties, he argues, are among the clearest real-world manifestations of this process. More generally, the partial truth argument seems to be especially suitable for explaining the importance of free speech when it comes to moral and political issues, where disagreement is generally the norm, as opposed for example to scientific matters, where the truth often is, indeed, all on one side.

While Mill does not emphasise, in *On Liberty*, the ways in which speech can harm, he does not overlook them either. In a famous passage, he writes:

> An opinion that corn-dealers are starvers of the poor, or that private property is robbery, ought to be unmolested when simply circulated through the press, but may justly incur punishment when delivered orally to an excited mob assembled before the house of a corn-dealer, or when handed about among the same mob in the form of a placard. (Mill 2006, p. 64)

This example looks like what we would nowadays call 'incitement to hatred', whereby a speaker stirs up hatred or hostility in the audience against a bystander, possibly causing violence. While Mill's bystanders are relatively privileged corn dealers and property owners, contemporary laws against incitement to hatred are generally intended to protect vulnerable religious, ethnic or other minorities.

Other restrictions consistent with Mill's doctrine concern forms of free speech that invade a person's self-regarding liberty to determine her own life (within the bounds of the harm principle). According to a Mill scholar such as Jonathan Riley (2005), examples in this category include the malicious invasion of another person's privacy, libellous speech that damages a person's social reputation, and false advertising in which manufacturers exploit consumers' relative ignorance about their products. Exactly what justifies these restrictions raises difficult issues in Mill scholarship, but the general answer is that these types of speech not only harm others; they also contribute little or nothing to the process of discovering truths that people have an interest in knowing (cf. Brink 2008).

Thus, in a landmark US Supreme Court case in the early 1940s, a Jehovah's witness was accused of using 'fighting words' – that is, words that provoke an immediate and often violent reaction in the listener – against a police officer. The Court ruled that 'such utterances are no essential part of any exposition of ideas, and are of such slight social value as a step to truth that any benefit that may be derived from them is clearly outweighed by the social interest in order and morality' (*Chaplinsky v New Hampshire* 1942). It is worth noting that in all such cases the harm is relatively short term and directed at specific individuals, and thus easy to assess within Mill's consequentialist framework. Where harms are longer term and more diffuse, they raise, among other issues, questions about the responsibility of the speaker (Ten 1980), as we shall see in later chapters, when we discuss hate speech and pornography.

Mill's case for free speech has been attacked on various grounds. One common criticism is that he proposes an over-intellectualised model of free speech, in which the social world is narrowly represented as a seminar room populated by earnest searchers for truth (Haworth 1998, pp. 24–32; Barendt 2005, pp. 9–10). But how about, for example, football chants, racist jokes, picketing strikers, or graffiti that stake out a gang's territory (see McKinnon 2006, pp. 123–4)? This list might suggest that fewer things engage our deliberative capacities than Mill thinks. But perhaps more is covered by the truth discovery argument than appears at first glance. Perhaps football chants bring home to third parties how football is a 'way of life' for diehard supporters. Likewise, racist jokes are offensive and sometimes hateful, but they also tell us something about people's attitudes towards race and ethnicity – and these views may be called out and contested. The 'Fuck the Draft' slogan in protest against the Vietnam war, a slogan that the Supreme Court defended as protected speech in *Cohen v California* (1971), may have helped to stimulate debate about the ethics of that war among those who saw it (see Barendt 2005, p. 10).

A further issue is that Mill seems to rely on an overly optimistic view of the likely consequences of free speech. Permissive public debate may result not in human progress, as measured by the discovery of truth and the development of our deliberative capacities, but in the rise and spread of extremist and other harmful views, with potentially catastrophic consequences for liberal democracy. Nazi Germany, for example, emerged from the thoroughly liberal Weimar Republic, and there are many recent examples of populism and far-right extremism in Europe, the United States, India and elsewhere, all spreading through a culture of free speech. Populist movements are often marked by the phenomenon of groupthink and a culture of intolerance; they do not consist of citizens who dispassionately think through the issues for themselves (and the same may be true to some extent of liberal regimes, too). Of course, whether speech should be limited in order to protect people's rights and other interests is a large and much contested question, as we will see in detail in later chapters. But Mill's view is particularly susceptible to the problem of the spread of harmful speech, and this is for two reasons.

First, unlike the autonomy and democracy arguments (which we will consider in a moment), Mill's future-oriented consequentialist approach tells us that the value of free speech lies in its results, and more specifically in its positive effect on enlightened human progress. If this does not happen, if a positive effect is not registered, his theory falters. Second, as a utilitarian interested in human happiness, Mill seemingly should be concerned with other sources of human utility besides the achievement of better justified views and opinions. The fear, insecurity, discrimination and sometimes violence that vulnerable ethnic, religious or sexual minorities suffer as a result of hate speech significantly undermine the well-being of these groups; surely they, too, should count when it comes to assessing the consequences of freedom of speech? Conversely, racist, Islamophobic, anti-Semitic, homophobic and other forms of harmful speech probably serve group solidarity and the identity formation of their illiberal authors, but should not these, too, count as sources of well-being, in the eyes of the consistent utilitarian? If so, Mill's consequentialist approach to free speech may seem less liberal than it appears at first glance.

Yet very often Mill is correct: the best way to combat false or harmful speech is, frequently, with more speech. Few of us think that people who deny the reality of human-caused climate change, or maintain that essential vaccines spread harmful illnesses, or argue that the COVID-19 pandemic was caused by 5G mobile phone masts[1] should be actively censored by the state or by social media, although there may be a case for not giving them a prominent platform (e.g. on television). To that extent, most of us are good Millians: we think that false speech should be addressed with reason and evidence rather than silenced.

Free speech and autonomy

Autonomy involves a person's governing her life according to her own judgement of what is best. It is opposed to a state in which some other agents usurp or thwart that judgement and direct the person's life themselves. Such agents might be individuals (e.g. a slave owner, or a controlling husband who runs his wife's life), groups (e.g. a religious hierarchy that directs every aspect of its adherents' lives) or the state, which has the capacity coercively to require that citizens live in a certain way. Although there are affinities between autonomy and Mill's ideal of individuality, the relationship between autonomy and free speech is more complex than in Mill's truth-based account, for at least two reasons. First, it has been proposed in different ways by different contemporary writers; second, we need to attend more carefully to the distinctions between deontological and consequentialist models and between speaker- and audience-based views. A further distinction is between formal and substantive theories of autonomy (Baker 2011, pp. 253–4). Substantive autonomy is a character ideal – namely the ideal of self-government, which a person may realise in her life. Formal autonomy implies that third parties respect a person's right to conduct her life according to her own best judgement.

Formal autonomy may be speaker-based or audience-based – that is, based on respect for a person's capacity to express her views or on respect for an audience's right to hear everyone's view – but, either way, it is deontological rather than consequentialist in character. It implies that third parties are prevented from interfering in individuals' lives (in our case, by having their speech limited), when they may want to do so for reasons of their own or for paternalistic ones – for example if they think that they could improve people's lives by preventing them from accessing material they consider morally reprehensible. The only valid reason for interfering with a person's formal autonomy, on this argument, is to protect the formal autonomy of another when that person would otherwise fail to respect it herself. (Here there is a clear affinity with Mill's harm principle.)

Since we certainly need speech (ours and others') in order to govern our own lives, the way autonomy can ground a defence of free speech is clear. A number of free speech theorists have adopted this strategy. One of the foremost American legal commentators on free speech, the late C. Edwin Baker (1997, 2011), proposed a speaker-based view that emphasises how (substantive) autonomy involves disclosing one's own beliefs to a social world we share with others. Respect for autonomy, for Baker, 'requires that each person must be permitted to be herself and to present herself [to others]. She must be permitted to act in and sometimes affect the world by at least some means, in particular by trying to persuade or criticize others' (Baker 1997, p. 992). Respect for free speech, as part of respect for autonomy, protects people's capacity to interact with one another on their own terms.

In another influential version of the argument, the late American legal philosopher Ronald Dworkin argued for a 'right to moral independence', which closely resembles respect for the formal autonomy of speakers and of audiences (see Brison 1998, pp. 324–5). According to Dworkin,

> People have the right not to suffer disadvantage in the distribution of social goods and opportunities, including disadvantage in the liberties permitted to them by the criminal law, just on the ground that their officials or fellow-citizens think that their opinions about the right way for them to lead their own lives are ignoble or wrong. (Dworkin 1981, p. 194)

Here the reference to opportunity and liberty incorporates freedom of speech. Dworkin's target was authorities who wished to regulate the availability of pornography because they considered it base or sinful, or thought that people's lives would go better if they did not view pornography.

But the most philosophically elaborate formal autonomy view is provided by another philosopher, T. M. Scanlon (1972), in a quite old but much cited article. For Scanlon, respecting formal autonomy involves respecting a person's sovereignty in deciding what to believe and what to do in light of what she hears, sees or reads; so his is an audience-based theory. In contrast to Dworkin, Scanlon is concerned with individuals who might go on to commit harms against others on the basis of speech they receive. According to him,

> There are certain harms which, although they would not occur but for certain acts of expression, nonetheless cannot be taken as part of a justification for legal restrictions on these acts. These harms are: (a) harms to certain individuals which consist in their coming to have false beliefs as a result of those acts of expression; (b) harmful consequences of acts performed as a result of those acts of expression, where the connection between the acts of expression and the subsequent harmful acts consists merely in the fact that the act of expression led

the agents to believe (or increased their tendency to believe) these acts to be worth performing. (Scanlon 1972, p. 213)

Suppose I calmly tell you that Jews control our country's financial system, that Muslims are all terrorists, or that our country's gay teachers are trying to 'make' our children gay. All three views are false. But this fact cannot justify censoring my speech, because it is *you*, as an autonomous agent, who holds the right to decide what to believe. As Scanlon puts it in speaking of someone who has heard harmful views, '[t]he contribution to the genesis of his action made by the act of expression is, so to speak, superseded by the agent's own judgment' (Scanlon 1972, p. 212). However, if you were already an anti-Semite, Islamophobe or homophobe – that is, you already had those wrongful beliefs – and I urged you to attack one of these groups, or, even worse, if you had already decided to attack them and I gave you key information helping you to do so, that would be a different matter: in such cases my speech could be legitimately restricted. But, to use one of Scanlon's examples, Martin Luther, who nailed his 95 theses to the door of the Wittenberg Cathedral, thus starting the Protestant Reformation, could not be held responsible for the bloody religious wars that resulted from that major schism within the Christian world.

For some people, this will be counterintuitive. If you are the victim of a hate attack, you might well believe that you have the right to complain not just against your attacker but also against the person or group that fed him with prejudice and bigotry. Your attacker is morally responsible for what he did, but he acted in certain circumstances, and – even if this is difficult to prove – might have not acted in their absence. The agents responsible for engineering those circumstances, for example by creating extremist websites, arguably bear some responsibility too. Unlike Scanlon, then, we often think that speech that prompted individuals to commit harm should be regulated in some way.

A further issue with the autonomy theory is that it is relatively indiscriminating in that it does not offer especially stringent protection for certain kinds of high-value speech (see Sunstein 1993, pp. 141–3). From the perspective of autonomy, a view is a view that we have the right to receive or to express. But, like Mill, many thoughtful people today attach special value to speech about moral, religious, political, historical, scientific, cultural or artistic matters. Suppose, for example, that a government concerned about mitigating the effects of climate change banned airlines from advertising on television, radio, the Internet and print media in the same way in which, for public health reasons, it currently bans cigarette manufacturers from advertising. Compare that with a government that, concerned about its re-election prospects, sought to ban from those same media all discussion of an opposition party or movement. For everyone who values democracy, there seems to be something intuitively much more troubling about that second ban. But, from the perspective of respect for autonomy, it is less clear how the political ban is worse.

For most people who value autonomy, what really matters is not just its formal but also its substantive dimension – the ideal of individuals realising their capacity to chart their own lives. After all, it might be argued, there is little point in respecting a capacity that few people ever realise, if any at all. On the substantive view, personal autonomy is the ideal that individuals critically evaluate the cultural resources around them, including the speech of others, in order to choose and pursue those aims that they endorse. Since, in order to live self-directed lives, we also need to speak to others, the substantive view supports free speech both from the perspective of audiences and from that of speakers themselves.

There are, however, two large issues that stand in the way of a close connection between speech and substantive autonomy. One is that much speech bypasses or even subverts the capacity for critical reflection that lies at the heart of the ideal of substantive autonomy; thus, on the deontological view, it fails to respect this capacity or, on the consequentialist view, it fails to promote it. In a self-critique of his 1972 article, Scanlon draws attention to how some of the speech we are exposed to as audiences may not always help us to be 'sovereign in deciding what to believe and in weighing competing reasons for action' (Scanlon 1979, p. 531). 'Expression is a bad thing', he writes, 'if it influences us in ways that are unrelated to relevant reasons, or in ways that bypass our ability to consider these reasons' (p. 525).

Deceptive and subliminal advertising are clear examples of speech that bypasses our rational autonomy in order to persuade us to think and act in certain ways. And so are, arguably, certain types of food labels or forms of expression that are used as nudges, to '[s]ystematically [exploit] non-rational factors that influence human decision-making' (Hausman and Welch 2010). We might also think that a diet of fake news, as a result of which individuals are continually exposed to false views for which there is no evidence, undermines these individuals' capacity to assess critically what they hear, see and read. (We return to the issue of fake news in Chapter 6.) As Susan Brison has argued, hate speech, too, can undermine audiences' and bystanders' capacity for autonomy by leading them to acquire false beliefs such as that they are inferior and by undermining their self-esteem, both of which damage the capacity to reflect critically on one's surroundings (Brison 1998, pp. 326–8).

The other problem with the substantive view is that many people are not (or do not want to be) autonomous in the sense described by the ideal presented here. Consider a person who enters a closed religious order, where every aspect of her life is governed by strict rules interpreted and administered by religious elders. For such a person, free speech may still be important because it allows her to participate in religious prayer or other rituals; indeed these seem especially important and valuable forms of speech, but not because they involve the exercise of autonomous capacities. Or imagine a person who is a slave to peer pressure and craves approval from others so much that she follows the lead of her friends and family in every important life decision. Such a person does not seem to be very autonomous either, but most of us would argue that free speech is equally necessary for her. Perhaps relatively few people employ critical reflection and self-conscious choice in the way autonomy demands; nor does it seem necessarily wrong to reject autonomy. If the ideal of autonomy is 'sectarian' and autonomy as a fundamental good is 'an idea about which there is much reasonable controversy' (Cohen 1993, p. 222) in diverse societies, then according to many liberals it may not be politically legitimate for the state to protect free speech on its basis (cf. Rawls 2005 and Bonotti 2015).

Faced with this lack of connection between free speech and autonomy, a number of contemporary writers have sought to define some central interests of persons – capacities that, if realised, enable all people's lives to flourish – which are more closely related to free speech.

Jonathan Gilmore, for example, has argued that articulating our views to others is part of the very process of coming to form and understand our own ideas, judgements, opinions and beliefs in the first place (Gilmore 2011; cf. Garton Ash 2016, pp. 73–4). Likewise, the American philosopher Seana Valentine Shiffrin sets out a number of interests people have, namely in theoretical and practical thought, in exercising their imagination, in becoming distinct, authentic individuals with identities of their own, in acting as responsible moral agents, in living among other people, with all the mutual social influence that this involves, and in being recognised by others as persons with their own views (Shiffrin 2011, pp. 289–97). Like Gilmore, she also posits an interest in understanding the contents of our own minds. All these interests require free speech for their realisation. Shiffrin categorises her theory as belonging to the autonomy family (pp. 283, 297–303) but, unlike in the sectarian version of that view, her interests involve 'sparer assumptions' (p. 298), which seem more genuinely universal.

Free speech and democracy

The connection between democracy and free speech is intuitive. One cannot really imagine a democratic society without reasonably widespread free speech, and empirically democracies invariably do a better job of protecting free speech than dictatorships. Free speech in the public sphere enables parties to assemble coalitions of supporters, allows the opposition in legislatures to cross-examine the government, helps to mobilise protest movements, and gives citizens the liberty to criticise governments and to seek to shape public opinion. These more specific connections can be interpreted in consequentialist terms. On this view, free speech is a necessary instrument that allows democracies to flourish;

without it, democratic life withers away. There may be something to this argument, but free speech seems to be a constituent of democratic culture, not merely an instrument to achieve it: democracy and free speech are not analytically separable in the way in which truth and free speech are in Mill's consequentialist argument. Hence the connection between democracy and free speech seems deontological more than consequentialist.

The first writer to make explicit the connection between free speech and democracy was Alexander Meiklejohn, in his 1948 book *Free Speech and Its Relation to Self-Government.* Like other US scholars after him, Meiklejohn was concerned with interpreting that country's constitutional tradition. From the 1776 US Declaration of Independence he drew the lesson that no one should be called upon to obey a law unless he or she (originally, of course, only he) had a share in making it (Meiklejohn 1948, pp. 10–11). Being bound by laws that limit your liberty, when those laws arose from a process in which you had a say, is legitimate in a way in which being bound by laws that emanated from elsewhere is not. Meiklejohn was impressed by the vigorous political debate practised in local town meetings in New England in the north-eastern United States, a tradition that continues to some extent to this day. Town meetings are a form of direct democracy. Local citizens come together to debate and decide on policy priorities for their area. For Meiklejohn, apparent limits on free speech in those meetings were in fact a means of enabling it. If a community is divided over whether to adopt some controversial proposal, for example, it seems fair to give those who propose it and those who oppose it an equal amount of time to make their case and to take questions from the audience. There is a sense in which the equality rule limits each side's freedom of speech, as would curtailing the speech of a very long-winded audience member who wanted to take up all the time for himself; but in fact these rules are all in the service of the ideal of democratic free speech. 'What is essential', writes Meiklejohn, 'is not that everyone shall speak, but that everything worth saying shall be said' (p. 25). Free speech cannot be the right to say whatever one wants, to whomever one pleases on whatever occasion it pleases one to say it – a truth that the autonomy view may find a little harder to accommodate. By yoking free speech to democratic debate, Meiklejohn gives it a compelling defence and suggests a framework by which it may be regulated.

At the same time though, as we know, democracies can limit free speech. Democracies have banned books, censored media and limited extremist – or, to put it less charitably, radical – political speech. How does this square with the democratic defence of free speech? Here it is important to emphasise the discursive component in Meiklejohn's view. Democracy is not simply a process that takes citizens' views in the form of their votes and converts the latter via the principle of majority rule into representative government, local or national. As in the town meeting, so in society at large, democracy involves widespread vigorous discussion. Deliberative democracy, to use the contemporary label, has been the object of sustained critical attention from democratic theorists in the last thirty years. It involves widespread rational, critical debate where citizens articulate the reasons behind their views, often emphasising how these reasons may be acceptable to others. Typically, the aim is to build consensus and reach agreement. The idea is that political decisions are more legitimate and morally defensible when they have been subject to vigorous challenge and counter-challenge. Deliberative theorists contrast their view with a simple voting procedure whereby, shielded by the secrecy of the ballot, citizens may vote on the basis of misguided, ill-informed, prejudiced, irrational or morally obnoxious reasons; yet these theorists do not deny that voting is usually necessary in decision-making in all but the smallest scale. Deliberative bodies are increasingly being used in many liberal democracies in order to involve citizens in processes of deliberation and consultation that will then affect the decisions of their representatives. They are often called 'mini-publics' (Setälä and Smith 2018) or 'citizens' assemblies' (Warren and Pearse 2008). One worry about the deliberative democratic ideal is its relatively demanding nature; another one, not unrelated, is that in practice deliberation will privilege more advantaged citizens, who are often better able to articulate their views (for an overview of these debates see Bächtiger et al. 2018).

Although these two concerns are real, conceptualising democracy in deliberative terms goes a long way towards addressing the issues posed by representative democracies that limit free speech. On the deliberative view, free speech is the lifeblood of a democratic political culture; thus, in limiting it too severely, actual democracies would not properly respect their own normative ideal. Even if contemporary constitutional democracies in Europe, North America, Australasia and elsewhere fall some way short of the deliberative democratic ideal, the fact that they invariably give free speech constitutional protection bespeaks a degree of understanding of the notion that free speech is constitutive of a democratic political culture. At the same time, democratic free speech is compatible with, indeed may demand, some limits beyond the regulatory ones we have noted. For example, hate speech that claims that members of a minority ethnic or religious group are not genuinely members of the political community disrespects that group's right to participate in the democratic process; for that reason hate speech might be regulated.

Contemporary free speech theorists who have adopted the democratic view have defended a largely speaker-centric approach. For Robert Post, the value of democratic rule lies not so much in informed decision-making as in citizens' ability reasonably to regard themselves as the ultimate authors of the law. This 'requires that citizens have access to the public sphere so that they can participate in the formation of public opinion' (Post 2011, p. 482) as well as hold their governments accountable to that opinion. This view sees free speech as the counterpart of formal voting, which (directly) puts in place a government and (indirectly) influences citizens' attitudes in the public domain. Free speech seeks to shape citizens' views, an important feature of democracy and something that elected governments always have an eye on.

A similar view is advanced by James Weinstein, who asserts 'an uncontestable right of each individual to free and equal participation in the political process, including the public discussion by which our society's laws, policies, and norms are evaluated' (Weinstein 2011, p. 505). Weinstein connects the right to public speech with the value of political legitimacy. Just as it is illegitimate for unelected governments to make law and policy, so the decisions of fully elected governments are illegitimate, according to Weinstein, unless every citizen is free to speak out in favour of or against them (p. 498). It is this, according to Weinstein, which explains the cardinal US First Amendment principle of viewpoint neutrality: that it is always illegitimate for governments to limit the expression of any particular view or opinion, however controversial. (We consider the implications of Weinstein's position for hate speech in the next chapter.)

In his book *Democracy and the Problem of Free Speech*, the legal theorist Cass Sunstein defends another democracy-based argument for free speech by drawing an explicit distinction between 'upper tier' (high-value) speech, which contributes to public deliberation, and 'lower tier' speech, which does not. The upper tier category is capacious: apart from overtly political speech, it includes artistic, literary and cultural critique and broader social commentary (Sunstein 1993, pp. 148–53). Upper tier speech merits especially strong protection – that is, not just through viewpoint neutrality but also through the more encompassing content neutrality, which forbids governments from regulating speech merely on the grounds that it covers contentious topics, regardless of the view that is expressed on them. Thus, if a company forbade its employees to post any political views on social media, it would violate the constraint of content neutrality. Only content-neutral restrictions on the time, place and manner in which one expresses oneself may on occasion be justified at the level of upper tier speech. Thus it might be legitimate, for example, for a company to bar employees from posting political views on social media during work hours.

The lower tier category consists of all other speech, including commercial speech (e.g. product descriptions, advertising), scientific speech, unlicensed medical and legal advice, depictions of violence in the media, defamation, hate speech, at least some pornography (some of which might also be political, as we shall see in Chapter 5), criminal speech such as bribery, insider trading, perjury, and threats of injury. This is a slightly confusing category, because it includes speech that is, actually or potentially, harmful in various ways and might even be better classified as conduct, not speech (e.g. threats and bribery), and speech that is not harmful but is not political either, even in the most expansive sense.

At any rate, the question is whether focus on political speech, broadly considered, is a strength or a weakness of the democratic view. The case for the latter is that there are certainly some kinds of intuitively high-value speech that are not political (or are political only if everything else is, which makes that category uninformative). Scientific speech is one example. Perhaps some of it is political – speech about climate change, for example – but much is not (e.g. pure mathematics), and anyway we might distinguish, say, between the science of climate change and its political implications. The religious speech of a closed religious order, such as the Amish or ultra-orthodox Jews, is another example. Speech on intimate matters between partners, family and friends is yet another. But, as we noted at the start, free speech often means in effect free *public* speech, something that these three forms normally are not. Given that there are rights to academic freedom, to freedom of religious conscience, and to a private life that will protect speech in these areas, is it enough if the democratic view explains only the value of public speech?

Indeed the argument from democracy has an important advantage. In a liberal society there is always a presumption in favour of individual liberty, unless such liberty interferes with the interests of others. By helping us to distinguish between political speech (broadly interpreted) and non-political speech, the democracy argument explains why it may often be more permissible to regulate the latter than to regulate the former. As Robert Post notes, for example, an attack on the reputation of a public figure might fairly be seen as a contribution to political debate in a way in which defamation of a private individual is not (Post 2011, p. 480). The latter is a potential civil wrong. By contrast, the US Supreme Court upheld the former doctrine in *New York Times Co. v Sullivan* (1964), where that newspaper published an advert critical of the behaviour of the police in Alabama, which had arrested Martin Luther King Jr, as well as in other cases since then. In general, political speech may be more important to protect just by virtue of its connection with state power, and therefore with our other rights and freedoms.

Interconnections between the three theories

Are the three theories examined in this chapter alternatives? Could we not endorse them all? There seems to be no reason to think that free speech cannot have multiple foundations (Greenawalt 1989), but at the same time we should be careful. Any justification for free speech also shapes our view of its limits; indeed, that is part of its point. While the autonomy theory is probably the most capacious, the truth theory has a harder time protecting free speech unconnected to the search for truth – much hate speech or commercial speech, for example – while on the democratic view hate speech could be taken as a contribution to democratic debate, or perhaps as undermining it, if it impedes others' participation. In the chapters that follow we discuss in greater detail what these divergent implications are. To conclude this chapter, we say something briefly from the converse perspective. How are these theories related?

As we noted above, there is a clear affinity between Mill's ideal of individuality and the ideal of personal autonomy. It is individualists who are most interested in truth in public affairs, and the search for truth, though a very social one – it must involve dialogue – is also one where individuals must exercise their independent critical powers by evaluating others' views, by offering their own judgement to others, and by deciding what to believe. This is not the whole of autonomy – a person could conceivably exercise her deliberative capacities in the weighty public matters with which Mill was concerned, yet always follow the crowd in her personal life – but it is a substantial part of it. Conversely, the autonomous person has an interest in truth even in aspects of her life that are not public or political. A young woman contemplating a career in law or finance, for instance, has an interest in knowing which of those two professional fields is more marked by sex discrimination.

As far as the relationship between autonomy and democracy is concerned, there seems to be a clear analogue between the ideal of a person charting her own future and that of a political society doing the same thing. The democratic society should not be bound any more than the autonomous person by customs, norms, traditions or conventions that are beyond critical interrogation, revision, and sometimes even rejection. (The 2018 referendum in Ireland that we mentioned at the start, in which the Irish people voted to repeal the abortion ban rooted in its Catholic heritage, is a case in point.) The ideal of deliberative democracy, in particular, requires that individuals consider issues for themselves and exchange views on political matters. If, by contrast, we thought that democracy simply meant that each party should mobilise its base, appeal to people's prejudices, and make them vote in secret without sharing their reasons, then democracy would not have much to do with autonomy, although, even on this pared-down view, it would still involve some free speech. As receivers of speech, we could also develop a democratic version of Scanlon's autonomy argument. The idea would be that citizens cannot make informed rational decisions on matters of public concern unless they have had the opportunity to receive information from divergent viewpoints. It is not difficult to see how this argument could be developed to support pluralism in the media, for example, as well as a strict doctrine of content neutrality.

What about the relationship between truth and democracy? Recent work in democratic theory has explored its epistemic dimension, the way in which democratically made decisions are likely to be more cogent or well founded than decisions made by a small cabal. Although he defends this view, David Estlund (2008) also gives serious consideration to what he calls 'epistocracy' – that is, government exercised by those most likely to arrive at correct decisions, like the Guardians in Plato's *Republic*. Conversely, given universal education, a public culture of deliberation, and the unique perspective on the world that is the preserve of every person, one might think that there is strength in numbers. Just as ten scientists working collaboratively are more likely to solve a puzzle than one working alone, the corporate body of citizens working together is better able to figure out what is in the public interest than a small epistocratic elite would. (This is in fact Estlund's argument for democracy.) Of course, how far citizens really work together in a democracy is a moot point. The thoughtful, civic-minded model of the democratic process defended by deliberative theorists is far removed from the adversarial and populist democracy found across the globe. Much the same can be said about free speech itself; often disrespected, it remains an ideal – for the sorts of reasons we have canvassed in this chapter.

2
Hate Speech

Introduction

A newspaper prints derogatory slurs about Muslim citizens authored by its star columnist; an online political forum becomes a magnet for anti-Semitic abuse; signs appear across a university that insult the intelligence of its black students; a disabled employee is subject to systematic harassment at work, including through verbal assaults; a prominent politician gives a widely viewed speech in which he describes recent migrants as vermin. Do these examples look like hate speech? If they do – and this is a separate question – should their proponents be punished or reprimanded in some way, or should they merely be exposed to general social stigma? Given the harms of hate speech, should states, social media organisations, employers, universities and other actors regulate or even censor it in some way?

Probably no topic in the recent literature on free speech has received as much commentary as hate speech. Moreover, in the past two decades countless online forums have emerged, multiplying the opportunities for hateful language – which is often proffered anonymously, with little premeditation – and become available almost instantaneously to a potentially very large audience (e.g. Brown 2018; Cohen-Almagor 2015). The rise of far-right and populist movements across many parts of the world has intensified the pervasiveness of hate speech both online and offline, prompting warnings of the emergence of a 'transnational extreme-right' (Davey and Ebner 2019, p. 4).

After providing some preliminary remarks on the meaning of hate speech, its different varieties, and the contexts where it applies, we discuss in this chapter what the three approaches to free speech presented in Chapter 1 – autonomy, truth and democracy – imply for hate speech. We then consider in greater detail the strengths and weaknesses of four further arguments in favour of hate speech regulation – namely that it assaults people's dignity, attacks their reputation, undermines their social participation, and harms their basic interests. We conclude by taking a closer look at some of the reasons for resisting hate speech regulation, specifically the difficulty of crafting hate speech laws that are neither under- nor overinclusive; and we examine alternatives to proscribing hate speech such as counterspeech and social integration.

Understanding hate speech

Hate speech has been characterised as a manifestation of basic disrespect and as an assault on dignity and human rights. It is believed to inflame violence, criminality and public disorder and to create an intolerant climate of hate; to convey insulting, offensive, abusive, vilifying and contemptuous messages; to degrade, demean, humiliate, subordinate and stigmatise those whom it targets; and to compound the discrimination, marginalisation and everyday harassment suffered by vulnerable groups (see Brown 2015; Strossen 2018, pp. 108–9). It is important to recognise that each of these harms is subtly different from the others and therefore that these views construe hate speech in diverse ways. It is also important to separate the issue of what hate speech is – a matter of how we define it – from the question of the effects it *causes*.

On the definitional issue, we suggest that the key feature of hate speech – as understood in legal and political theory and in much hate speech legislation – is that its language or symbols deliberately and foreseeably attack the basic civic standing of the groups it targets. Hate speech communicates that, on account of their group identity, those who belong to certain groups are not genuine members of society; in this way hate speech amplifies these groups' marginalisation or subjection to discrimination, domination, oppression and the like, or at least their systemic vulnerability to those wrongs.[1] Hate speech successfully attacks individuals *as group members*; but, for it be successful and therefore count as hate speech, it must exploit a pattern or structure of prior injustices. It is in the augmentation of these injustices that the harms of hate speech lie. This being so, it cannot be employed against members of majority or privileged groups; it lacks the normative traction to harm them (at least in any significant way). As Delgado and Stefancic (1994, p. 782), put it, 'hate speech directed against blacks and other minority groups has no ready analog in speech against whites ... Whites may suffer words of criticism, envy, and so on, but there really is no such thing as hate speech directed against them.' One can be *hateful*, in one's speech, towards a member of a fortunate or advantaged group without its being *hate speech*. For similar reasons, the category of hate speech makes little sense when hate is focused on a person purely on the basis of her or his individual characteristics. If I say 'John is a total scumbag who doesn't deserve to live', that is hateful, but does not constitute hate speech because 'scumbag' is a term of abuse, not a social category of persons subject to injustice. If someone says 'Jews are vermin', that is hate speech: vermin are 'dirty' creatures we want to drive out. If, in social circumstances where John's Jewishness is significant and salient, someone says 'John is vermin; he doesn't belong here', that is probably hate speech, assuming that the speaker is exploiting that context to target John *as a Jew* (even if only implicitly).

Clearly the brief definition we are dealing with here leaves grey areas open, though this is not by itself a disadvantage, since hate speech is partly dependent on context. But at the same time defining hate speech as a successful attack on a person's civic status, carried out on the basis of her group membership when that group is underprivileged, has some substance to it. It helps to distinguish hate speech from offensive speech, which does not necessarily involve an assault on people's status (though, as we will see in Chapter

4, there are grey areas there as well). It also rules out the possibility that members of majority groups are victims of hate speech. If someone says 'Whites are scum!' in a majority-white society, that is hateful language but not hate speech; the desire to rid society of white people or deprive them of equal civic status, though logically coherent, gains no purchase in a majority-white population, or even in one where whites constitute an advantaged minority, as in apartheid South Africa (cf. Waldron 2012, p. 237, note 13).

Hate speech, we suggested, is commingled with the wider injustices to which society's more vulnerable members are subject: incivilities and micro-aggressions (McTernan 2018); poor housing, crime-ridden neighbourhoods and civic segregation; lack of a democratic voice; structural lack of opportunities in education and employment; and harassment and discrimination more generally. These injustices invite reflection on the question of which groups exactly hate speech laws are designed to protect. Minority ethnic groups (e.g. African Americans, South Asian and African immigrants in Europe and their descendants) and religious minorities (e.g. Muslims and Jews in Europe and elsewhere) are, typically, the categories envisaged by advocates of regulation.

However, ethno-religious minorities are not the only groups protected by hate speech rules, existing or proposed. Other relevant groups include LGBTIQ+ people; individuals with mental or physical disabilities; recent immigrants and refugees, even when not ethnically or religiously distinct (e.g. many EU citizens in the United Kingdom); Travellers and Roma people; and the poor and indigent. To give one example with LGBTIQ+ people, in 2015, when the feminist writer Germaine Greer publicised the view that transgender women 'are not women',[2] an online petition asking Cardiff University to cancel a scheduled lecture by Greer stated that, '[w]hile debate in a university should be encouraged, hosting a speaker with such problematic and hateful views towards marginalised and vulnerable groups is dangerous'.[3] (We turn to the specific policy of no-platforming in Chapter 6.) Some have claimed that epithets such as 'white trash', directed at the white working class, might to some extent constitute instances of hate speech (e.g. Barendt 2005, p. 175), because in countries such as the United States these people, too, have suffered from historical injustice and marginalisation. Women might also be included qua women. While not a minority group, they often are subject to discrimination and various forms of unfair treatment, and this makes them potential victims of hate speech. All the above categories plainly overlap and cut across each other.

Besides the meaning of hate speech and the categories of people it targets, it is also important to understand what its *regulation* involves. In many cases, hate speech laws are state-sanctioned. However, hate speech regulation may apply beyond the public realm. In the workplace, for example, employees may be subject to rules on speech that are more stringent than regular laws and govern what they may communicate, both internally and with clients. Colleges and universities may similarly adopt hate speech codes that govern interactions between and among staff and students and are intended to safeguard a diversity of viewpoints, promote inclusivity, and protect an ethos of free and open inquiry. To repeat, these measures tend to be more restrictive than the laws that apply to society generally. The rationale for imposing such restrictions is, in part, that individuals choose to enter these institutions – in other words enter them out of their own will – or are distinctly vulnerable as a result of their membership.

Beyond that, France, Austria, Ireland and some other European countries have hate speech legislation that can apply even to small gatherings and in someone's home, in a way that would be anathema in the United States and, in principle, would leave no secure private refuge for the hateful (Strossen 2018, pp. 112–13). Public television and other broadcasters may have particular statutory duties related to avoiding stereotypical and discriminatory messages (e.g. Brown 2015, p. 22).

By far the largest censors of hate speech in liberal democratic societies, it is important to note, are private Internet corporations such as Google, Twitter and Facebook, where complex algorithms and moderators are involved in taking down content judged to violate their own free speech standards. The presence of largely unaccountable social media organisations also raises the important question of how far such companies are responsible for hosting hateful messages spread by private groups and individuals (Garton Ash 2016, p. 193, p. 238; see also Brown 2018). In the United States, social media companies are protected by Section 230 of the 1996 Communications Act, according to which they are not, legally, publishers of the content they host. Section 230 is controversial and has been subject to numerous legal challenges. Similarly, in June 2020 France's constitutional court struck down a law that would have forced online platforms to remove hateful content within 24 hours of its being flagged by users.[4] By contrast, the 2019 Online Harms White Paper in the United Kingdom set out the government's initial proposals for addressing harmful but often legal content on the Internet, particularly content aimed at young people – including online bullying and images of self-harm – as well as material that threatens national security or undermines social integration and shared rights and responsibilities.[5] Internet corporations such as Facebook would be overseen by an independent regulator endowed with the power to set and enforce rules on online speech – a dangerous, potentially arbitrary intrusion into speech according to its critics.

As far as state-sanctioned hate speech laws are concerned, while their ultimate rationale may be to prevent communicative assaults on vulnerable groups' civic standing, they exhibit a variety of legal features, thus testifying to the diversity of normative considerations that we mentioned earlier. In his study of the philosophical basis of hate speech laws, Alexander Brown (2015) very usefully catalogues these laws in a way we draw upon here. As he notes, sometimes laws proscribing the denial of acts of mass cruelty, violence or genocide such as the Holocaust are categorised as hate speech laws (we address Holocaust denial in the next chapter). In some US states, hate speech is categorised as denial of human rights such as the right to non-discrimination, as when a 'whites only' sign is posted above a restroom door in a workplace (*EEOC v Tyson Foods, Inc.* 2006). These instances raise difficult normative issues about the conflict between free speech and other rights and illustrate our earlier point that hate speech may be a component in larger illegal acts. Some states legislate against expression-oriented hate speech, for example against fighting words, as well as against non-verbal expression, such as a swastika painted in a Jewish neighbourhood or a burning cross (a threatening and intimidating symbol associated with the Ku Klux Klan) erected outside the homes of African Americans, and other race-based violence against them.[6]

Another cluster of hate speech laws more readily captures the status assault that is central to the phenomenon. These include laws against the negative stereotyping or stigmatisation of others. Such laws apply especially to public broadcasters, which normally have a duty of impartiality. Thus in 2009 Ofcom, the communications regulator in the United Kingdom, censured the popular radio presenter Chris Moyles for interpreting a song in a style that lampooned the singer Will Young's sexual orientation (this case is cited in Brown 2015, p. 22). In the United States, some states have laws against the kind of group defamation that hate speech seems to inflict on vulnerable groups. The landmark *Beauharnais v Illinois* (1952) case, for example, concerned a white supremacist distributing racist leaflets directed against black Americans. In its decision, the US Supreme Court deemed constitutional an Illinois law that, as it stated, 'makes it a crime to exhibit in any public place any publication which "portrays depravity, criminality, unchastity, or lack of virtue of a class of citizens, of any race, color, creed or religion" which "exposes the citizens of any race, color, creed or religion to contempt, derision, or obloquy"' (*Beauharnais v Illinois* 1952).

Along similar lines run hate speech laws that criminalise humiliating or degrading a person and robbing her of her dignity (without necessarily damaging her reputation). In a few instances, even in the United States, victims have successfully sued for damages on the basis of the emotional distress that resulted from dignity-based harms such as 'insults, slurs, evocations of the Ku Klux Klan, statements comparing black men to apes, death threats, and the placement of a noose dangling from the plaintiff's automobile' (*Turley v ISG Lackawanna, Inc.* 2014).

Another group of laws against hate speech proscribe it on the basis that it is an incitement to hatred of some kind. The 2006 Racial and Religious Hatred Act in the United Kingdom, for example, made it an offence to stir up hatred intentionally through threatening words or behaviour. Unlike laws that proscribe the mere expression of hateful speech, incitement laws direct their attention to hate-inspired acts that *others* may commit upon hearing hate speech or witnessing manifestations of it (see Scanlon 1972). Hate speakers instigate a series of events that may end in violence or other harms, but they need not be themselves involved in these harmful acts. As Nadine Strossen, a prominent critic of hate speech laws, maintains, hate speech affects its listeners and observers only via their 'intermediating perceptions', with the help of which it joins the jumble of other influences that cause people to commit harm (Strossen 2018, p. 22). For instance, RTLM (Radio Télévision Libre des Mille Collines), the Rwandan radio station run by the majority-Hutu community in that country, broadcast a barrage of anti-Tutsi propaganda in 1994, before the massacre of Tutsis by Hutus. But, although this propaganda counts as hate speech in the expressive meaning of that term, it is less clear, given pre-existing deep social tensions in Rwandan society, that such broadcasts were the (or even a) factor that incited the genocide (p. 66). Much the same can be said about laws and regulations that seek to prevent conduct that, in the view of legal authorities (e.g. the police), is likely to lead to public disorder, social unrest, damage to property and the like (Brown 2015, pp. 28–9).

Hate speech restrictions may operate within specific institutional contexts (workplace regulations, university speech codes or a media organisation's internal rules), may belong to state- or substate-level criminal and civil statutes, and may be condemned in principle by international conventions and declarations that lack specific legal force, such as the UN International Convention on the Elimination of All Forms of Racial Discrimination (ICERD) (Brown 2015, pp. 39–40; Strossen 2018, p. 108). Rather than focus on the specifics of these rules, our aim is to step back and examine the injustice of hate speech as such – and the normative basis (if any) of combatting that injustice. In the next section we show that none of the three general theories of free speech introduced in Chapter 1 gives unambiguous guidance on responding to hate speech.

Hate speech and truth

The consequentialist view we considered says that a free speech regime is particularly conducive to the discovery of true or justified answers to questions of value, as most famously argued by J. S. Mill. One might think that permitting the expression of hate speech, however painful, serves a valuable purpose because it encourages more reasonable citizens to show that hate purveyors are mistaken. Using argument and reason we could strengthen the general belief in ideals such as racial equality, when racist beliefs are exposed to the cold light of day. This would imply overcoming the 'dead dogma' attitude with which, according to Mill, we hold many of our beliefs, including those concerning racial equality and liberal democratic values more generally. In the long run, contesting hate speech in public might even persuade at least some hate-mongers to abandon their views in line with Mill's infallibility argument, according to which free speech can help us replace falsehood with truth.

However, the issues are less obvious than this picture suggests. For the Millian argument to succeed, participants in free speech debate should all plausibly have at least some minimal motivation to arrive at justified opinions. However, hate speakers who exchange views in echo chambers and Internet enclaves do not seem very interested in having their own views challenged; this conflicts with Mill's apparent assumption that participants in the practice of free speech are all committed to justifying their beliefs and values to others (especially to those they disagree with) and are all open to revising these beliefs and values.

Another objection to Mill's argument is that, if we have reasonable knowledge of the content of views that are contrary to our own, no one needs actually to express them in order to test our views against their competitors. This objection applies especially strongly to hate speech, given the hurt it causes. Since reasonable, non-racist citizens already know that a minority holds racist views, censoring any particular hateful utterance or writing does not seem to do much to disable those citizens' disinterested search for the truth. Still, one might respond that being *forced* to confront extremist views and to defeat them in argument strengthens our deliberative capacities to defend our beliefs and critique opposing ones.

However, for members of a vulnerable racial minority, being told that they must bear the brunt of racist bigots' verbal assault in order for their (and other citizens') deliberative capacities to be strengthened may not be much solace. Surely – they might respond – there are less harmful ways of strengthening these capacities? Further, one result of hate speech is that minority voices find their social authority to contribute to public discussion progressively eroded, so that they are less trusted as advocates in social practices of public deliberation; and they cease to be considered credible, competent and trustworthy contributors to public debate. In this way they also become victims of what is called 'epistemic injustice' (Fricker 2007). Finally, appealing to the importance of using our deliberative faculties in order to reject hate speech can only go so far. At least some forms of hate speech, for example fighting words, clearly hinder rather than foster our use of those faculties (Brink 2008). The landmark US Supreme Court decision *Chaplinsky v New Hampshire* (1942), which we mentioned earlier, said that fighting words 'by their very utterance inflict injury or tend to incite an immediate breach of the peace', but have only 'slight social value'.

Even if combatting some forms of hate speech does involve our deliberative faculties, this very attempt might, all things considered, hinder the discovery of truth. A case in point is discrimination against or harassment of certain ethnic groups that is based on alleged evidence of their lower IQ, where disproving the latter could in principle be the topic of a reasoned debate. As Brown (2015, p. 114) puts it, 'finding out the truth about certain groups or classes of persons is harder when one first has to wade through a quagmire of lies and false rumors than if one begins with a blank page, so to speak'.

Another, more general problem with the Millian defence of free speech is that it is too focused on truth as a human interest and component of well-being, at the expense of other interests that must enter the consequentialist calculation of what rules a society should adopt in order to maximise overall well-being (Schauer 2012). The kinds of harms we surveyed in the last section – reputational damage, disparagement, assaults on dignity and so on – are all 'bads' that a consistent consequentialist will want to reduce in designing society's legal and regulatory framework. That points to a policy of hate speech restrictions. Thus what the consequentialist argument for free speech really implies for hate speech depends very much on how we interpret many competing interests, values and disvalues and how much weight we give to each of them in different circumstances.

Hate speech and autonomy

Much the same occurs with arguments both for and against regulating hate speech, when we consider the autonomy-led approach to free speech (cf. Brown 2015, pp. 58–66). In Chapter 1 we outlined Scanlon's (1972) original autonomy-based justification for free speech, which focused on our interest in arriving at our own judgements of worth and value; and this is something for which we need a wide circulation of ideas, if we are to be able to do it. Applied to hate speech, Scanlon's autonomy argument supports two views that count against its legal regulation.

First, even though disparagement, defamation, and humiliating messages directed at vulnerable members of the political community are ill-founded, restrictions on hate speech illegitimately intrude upon individuals' sovereign right to determine for themselves those members' proper civic status. Second, we saw in the last section how laws can proscribe hate speech on the basis of the further harms it is said to incite, such as harassment, discrimination, violence, damage to property, and public disorder. But championing the value of personal autonomy, as Scanlon's argument does, places responsibility for these kinds of harms squarely on angry citizens, who have received hate speech from others and are thereby incited to commit them. If the standard of autonomy is upheld, it is *they* who are responsible for acting on the basis of what they see and hear. They should be justly punished for their criminal acts – but those who first engaged in hate speech should not – or not necessarily (but cf. Howard 2019).

C. Edwin Baker (1989, 2009, 2011) proposes a related autonomy-based argument against hate speech laws, this time appealing to the interests of speakers, not to those of the audience. According to Baker, autonomous individuals have the right to make choices and communicate their views and values to others, even if this involves using hateful or vituperative forms of speech. But Baker's critique of hate speech regulation goes further and also concerns state legitimacy. According to him, the state cannot reasonably ask the individuals under its dominion to obey the law unless it treats them as autonomous persons, able to make choices; and such treatment includes respect for the means of expression that these persons have chosen. Hate speech regulations fail to respect this principle, however, as they substitute the state's judgement for the individuals' judgement in matters of speech; hence they undermine the state's legitimacy.

Despite the apparent tension between individual autonomy and hate speech regulation, it may be permissible sometimes to restrict hate speech on autonomy-based grounds. As we saw in Chapter 1, Scanlon (1979) later pointed to ways in which free speech may subvert rather than respect its audiences' autonomous powers. Long-term exposure to hate speech, with its narrowness, distortions, stereotyping and slurs, seems more likely to undermine than to foster individuals' autonomous capacities for critical reflection, deliberation and judgement, though no doubt this effect will differ from person to person. This conclusion applies to third-party observers of hate speech, for example those who read the angry bile that is released on Internet news sites and social media against members of certain minorities. In other words, hate speech may sometimes exert 'undue influence' upon listeners (Brown 2015, p. 60), and this seems hardly conducive to the burdensome task of exercising one's capacity for independent judgement when it comes to directing one's own life. But, among the harms that hate speech visits on vulnerable minorities, the fact that it constitutes an assault on *their* ability to exercise personal autonomy is, plausibly, one of the most serious. In sum, though there are autonomy-based reasons to limit hate speech, given that hate speech is itself an exercise in personal autonomy, there are also reasons to permit it. Once we begin to think about autonomy less as a formal value or deontological constraint and more as a practical capacity that may be realised or thwarted in different political circumstances, its implications for hate speech regulation become far from clear.

Hate speech and democracy

Writers who endorse the democracy argument for free speech often argue that hate speech regulations would damage democracy in some way; but there are different ways in which this case can be made.

One version of the argument focuses on the concept of democratic legitimacy, which designates a state's right to make and enforce laws within its territory. There are competing accounts of what makes state authority legitimate, but one appealing view is that a state's promulgation of laws is legitimate if and only if citizens are free to participate 'upstream' – that is, if they are free to contribute to making these laws by participating, through free speech, in processes such as democratic deliberation in the public sphere about what 'downstream' (i.e. top-down) laws such as tax rules or traffic regulations should be (Weinstein 2017; Waldron 2017). Hence, according to the legal scholars Ronald Dworkin (2009), Robert Post (2011, 2017), and James Weinstein (2017), hate speech bans undermine democratic legitimacy: states lack the authority to enforce downstream laws against potential hate speakers whose speech has been curtailed upstream. As Jeremy Waldron (2017) points out, though, this argument seems to over-inflate the concept of legitimacy, which is not an individualised notion but rather a normative function of the political system as such. If one potential voter is wrongly disenfranchised, for example, that is an injustice and democracy is the poorer for it, but this occurrence does not by itself render that state illegitimate or imply that our thwarted voter is released from her obligation to obey the law.

Another version of the democratic argument against

hate speech bans focuses on the discursive dimension of democracy (Post 2011; Weinstein 2011; Heinze 2016). On this view, citizens who exercise their right to free speech are often seeking to influence public opinion and their political representatives. The wrong of hate speech bans is that they unjustifiably limit public debate and impede the participation of hate speakers in it. However outrageous or vituperative their views, hate speakers must be treated as equal citizens, with equal rights to political influence in a democracy.

But there are issues with this version of the democratic argument against bans too. First, it is far from clear that all hate speech can reasonably be regarded as a contribution to public debate. Episodic slurs in the public square, trolling on social media, or what Delgado calls 'the daily, low-grade largely invisible stuff, the hassling, cruel remarks, and other things' (Delgado 1991, p. 380 n. 319) look more like private acts; certainly they are intended to look that way by hate speakers and received as personal assaults by their victims. At the very least, this point renders the democratic argument inapplicable to a large proportion of hate speech.

Second and more fundamentally, regulating hate speech can sometimes augment rather than damage democratic debate. Just as it can set back the autonomy of vulnerable groups, hate speech can also impede their participation in social institutions and public life and erode other citizens' willingness to hear their political voice. Thus legally proscribing it could help members of minorities to contribute to public discourse themselves, and therefore help to realise the value of democratic legitimacy. If considerations such as these are correct, then liberal democratic states contemplating hate speech laws are somewhat caught in a bind, as either enforcing or not enforcing such laws will have deleterious consequences for democracy, and perhaps for legitimacy, too (Reid 2020).

Further arguments for hate speech regulation

In this section we examine some further arguments for hate speech regulation. An obvious starting point is the concept of harm, which, as we saw in Chapter 1, is central to Mill's political philosophy. When speech causes (or is likely to cause) harm to others, interfering with their legitimate interests and violating their rights, then regulating it may be permissible. How is Mill's harm principle relevant to hate speech?

Perhaps the clearest case is the one provided by instances of incitement to hatred. The 2006 Racial and Religious Hatred Act in the United Kingdom, we saw earlier, aimed to regulate precisely this category of hate speech. Incitement to hatred closely resembles what Mill had in mind in his corn dealer example. Inciting an angry mob to hate corn dealers by claiming that they are starvers of the poor is not unlike inciting, say, white working-class people to hate Muslim immigrants by accusing them of stealing jobs or exploiting the welfare state. As in Mill's example, the channel through which incitement to hatred is conveyed matters a good deal. If the leader of a white supremacist group holds a speech in a neighbourhood mainly inhabited by Muslims and incites his followers to hatred against them, then it is reasonable to presume that this may result in harms committed against the Muslims who live in the neighbourhood. However, the same speech conveyed, say, via a little-read Internet blog may not carry the same risk.

This also points to a second factor. Certain channels of incitement to hatred (e.g. those involving face-to-face contact between speaker and audience and physical proximity to potential victims) are more likely to lead to specific short-term harm, whereas others (e.g. online blogs and social media) may contribute to harm in the long term by creating a climate of hatred that fuels violence, injustice and discrimination, which are diffuse and episodic (see Brown 2008). But long-term predictions are more difficult to make, and negative effects can often be prevented by other means. Furthermore, intervening causal factors may reduce the speaker's responsibility, as it will be more difficult in their presence to establish how far it was *her speech* rather than broader social, cultural and economic processes – large-scale unemployment combined with high rates of immigration, for example – that led to hate and harm (see Ten 1980).

Another, perhaps narrower line of argument in defence of

hate speech regulation appeals to the fact that the victims of hate speech often suffer from a variety of health conditions as a result of being exposed to it – for example anxiety, depression, social withdrawal, alcoholism and high blood pressure (Brown 2015, pp. 56–7). However, once again, establishing a causal relationship is problematic (Heinze 2016; Strossen 2018), especially given that the minorities who are the target of hate speech are often already experiencing various injustices and burdens such as poverty, precarious employment, inadequate housing, crime-ridden neighbourhoods, police brutality, and discrimination and harassment, which may all affect their health negatively.

In order to avoid contentious claims about causal links, we could focus instead on what we claimed earlier to be the conceptual core of the phenomenon of hate speech, namely that it represents an assault on the civic status of those whom it targets – specifically, members of vulnerable minorities. As we noted, hate speech has sometimes been seen as a kind of group defamation; its intention, and often its effect, is to damage the public reputation of the ethnic or religious minorities it targets. Hence, this argument goes, just as we have laws against libel and slander directed at *individuals*, so hate speech regulations protect the public reputation of those groups that are targeted by hate speech. Crucially, public reputation (unlike private reputation, which is the target of libel and slander) is conceptually related to civic standing. For example, when President Trump, during the 2016 presidential campaign, said of Mexicans that '[t]hey're bringing drugs, they're bringing crime, they're rapists',[7] the implication was that most Mexicans in the United States do not belong to the community of law-abiding American citizens or non-American residents. *Beauharnais v Illinois* (1952) is a key legal case for the group defamation approach.

Other advocates of hate speech laws see hate speech as involving stigmatisation and an intention to demean. For example, the critical race theorist Richard Delgado (1982) argues that racial insults should qualify as a tort – a civil wrong whose victims could recover damages – and claims that hate speech is an 'affront to dignity'.[8] The notion of dignity is not really analysed, however, and, since it makes sense to say of someone that, despite being verbally assaulted by hate speech, he kept his dignity intact, the phrase 'affront to dignity' is relatively uninformative (cf. Brown 2015, pp. 91–2). Other critical race theorists adopt a more person-centred view of the harms that the subordinating nature of hate speech brings. Thus Mari Matsuda (1989, p. 2339), for example, maintains that the effect of racist hate propaganda is that, 'at some level, no matter how much both victims and well-meaning dominant-group members resist it, racial inferiority is planted in our minds as an idea that may hold some truth'. Charles Lawrence (1987, p. 351) claims instead that hate speech 'inflict[s] psychological injury by assaulting a person's self-respect'. Matsuda's and Lawrence's claims about hate speech's effect on human psychology are redolent of the points we made earlier about health.

A further kind of subordinating harm that hate speech plausibly inflicts on those it targets is that it silences them (cf. Brown 2015, pp. 84–6 and 198–200), either literally, because members of vulnerable minorities may be afraid of speaking back, or in what Miranda Fricker calls a testimonial sense (Fricker 2007). The latter claim is that hate speech helps maintain a social climate in which certain minority groups are not listened to, not trusted, or simply not heard no matter what they say. In the context of silencing, it is important to consider the authority of the hate speaker too. For example, hate speech used by a white legislator in apartheid South Africa (see Langton 1993, p. 302) might have threatened the black population more than hate speech by a random nobody on the street, given the legislator's power and authority, grounded in South Africa's constitution at the time. However, sometimes the specific context of an instance of hate speech matters too. For example, Maitra claims that an ordinary white man may succeed in ranking an Arab woman as inferior through his hate speech if bystanders remain silent (Maitra 2012, pp. 100–1; for a critique, see Brown 2015, pp. 78–9).

Not being socially silenced is, plausibly, also a basic interest of persons (to return to an earlier category), especially if such an interest is conceptualised more broadly, as related to effective social participation. So treated, this interest looks like a broader version of the democratic argument, which, as we saw earlier, can be marshalled in support of hate speech regulation. But this argument has been criticised on the grounds that there is a lack of convincing empirical evidence to substantiate it, as well as apparent counterevidence, for instance when victims of hate speech do speak back (Weinstein 2001; Brown 2015, pp. 198–200).

We finally consider what is perhaps the most theoretically plausible subordination-type argument for hate speech regulation: the one proposed by the Jeremy Waldron in his much discussed book *The Harm in Hate Speech* (Waldron 2012). Waldron's argument for hate speech regulation centres on the concept of dignity, but takes a somewhat different approach from that of Delgado and others. His focus is *civic*, as opposed to *human*, dignity, the former being the social rank or status accorded to different members of society. While defamation laws protect a person's individual reputation as the particular person she is, Waldron's interest is in our generic reputation as citizens of good standing. One great achievement of contemporary democratic societies has been to generalise and extend to all citizens the high rank previously awarded only to aristocrats and their ilk. In democratic societies today, we believe that citizens should not only enjoy equal legal rights, but also regard one another as equals: their civic status guaranteed by law should also be socially vindicated. This status is precisely what hate speech assaults.

Hate speech stigmatises those it attacks, impugning their equal status as citizens. When a hate speaker says that certain minorities are violent criminals, thieves, drug users or drug dealers, animals, or vermin, or that they should 'go back to their own country', or when, as has happened in the United States, signs outside a shop or restaurant say 'No Blacks Allowed', such acts undermine the reputation of members of those communities as citizens in good standing. Saying that all Muslims are thieves or terrorists, for example, implies that, simply as a result of their identity as Muslims, certain members of society should not be guaranteed the presumption of innocence, a fundamental legal right in any liberal democracy that is central to citizens' free and equal status. By contrast, a convicted thief or terrorist has damaged her own reputation, so if we call such a person a thief or a terrorist we are not ordinarily engaging in hate speech regardless of her group identity.

Moreover, Waldron points out that hate speech, much like wolves howling across a plain, calls out and emboldens other angry citizens, telling them, in effect, 'you are not alone, we hate them too' (Waldron 2012, p. 94). While eroding the public good of equal civic status, hate speech begins to replace it, for those in its frame, with the public bad of assaulted civic status. In a hate-saturated society, victimised minorities can no longer take for granted either the majority's commitment to justice or their own standing in the political community. It is this insecurity that hate speech laws address by providing the public good of 'assurance', the 'pervasive, diffuse, general, sustained, and reliable underpinning of people's basic dignity and social standing, provided by all to and for all' (p. 93). In other words, hate speech laws symbolically affirm the civic dignity of the victims of hate speech by publicly declaring that their society takes an official stand against its perpetrators.

Waldron's account of hate speech has been influential in recent discussions of the topic and has attracted considerable commentary. First, it is worth noting that Waldron's argument relies upon the successful application of hate speech laws in practice: where this fails, assurance will still be undermined – and, as we will shortly see, crafting and upholding hate speech laws faces considerable practical obstacles (Brown 2015, p. 149). Second, it is not entirely clear how the argument applies to groups whose members fail to enjoy the full schedule of civic rights and entitlements, such as resident non-citizens, who often are members of vulnerable racial or religious minorities and who, by definition, have a lower civic status (e.g. they generally do not have the right to vote or to access free healthcare or other welfare benefits), or citizens of other states, who may easily be targeted by online hate speakers even when physically very distant from them.

Third and most importantly, the key claim that hate speech undermines civic dignity can be read in two ways, each of them with an attendant problem. The most obvious reading of Waldron's argument is an empirical one, whereby hate speech laws are held to be necessary (if not sufficient) to maintain vulnerable minorities' civic dignity. Plausibly, civic dignity is also upheld by laws against discrimination, violence, harassment and other hate crimes, as well as by more general policies designed to improve minority groups' employment opportunities, media portrayal, social integration, civic participation, and so on. Furthermore, as we will see, counterspeech is another important non-censorial response to hate speech that the state may encourage. If measures such as these are all in place, it is less clear why hate speech laws in particular are *necessary* for cementing minorities' civic dignity; these other measures might, just by themselves, provide enough assurance to victims of hate speech in Waldron's sense (Simpson 2013; Brown 2015; Seglow 2016).

A less obvious interpretation of Waldron's argument holds it to be saying that hate speech itself *constitutes* an assault on civic dignity (Lepoutre 2017, pp. 857–8). On this view, Waldron would be making a conceptual claim about what hate speech *is* – such that 'dignity assault' would now be built into its definition – rather than a contingent claim about what hate speech *does*. But, if so, the relevance of how minorities themselves perceive such attacks is far less obvious; unlike in the empirical interpretation, their subjective perspective seems to have fallen out of the picture, in a way which seems counterintuitive.

Alternatives to hate speech regulation

Even if we accept the case for hate speech regulation in principle, a further issue is whether it is possible (a) to draft and enforce legislation that will outlaw the kinds of speech we want to censor while admitting other kinds of speech; and (b) to maintain the distinction between the two categories in a non-arbitrary way. In her fusillade against hate speech laws, Nadine Strossen (2018) is especially critical on this point. In her view, hate speech laws are almost inevitably vague, subjective and overbroad, and hence 'endow enforcing authorities with largely unfettered discretion to choose which ideas to single out for investigation and punishment' (p. 70). Moreover, given the common institutional biases, state authorities are more likely to censor the views of disempowered and marginalised groups, thus prejudicing their right to dissent (pp. 81–8), especially in states where democracy is already fragile. But even in established democracies, hate speech legislation has been used to silence unpopular dissenting views. For example, in 2012 a Muslim British teenager was arrested for his Facebook posts, which deplored British soldiers' killing of Afghan civilians (p. 84); likewise, in 2015, France's highest court upheld criminal convictions against twelve pro-Palestinian activists who wore T-shirts with the slogan 'Long live Palestine, boycott Israel' (p. 28). Besides such instances, the mere possibility that one is prosecuted under hate speech legislation arguably has an unwelcome, 'chilling' effect on potential speakers who hold radical, unorthodox, or simply politically unpopular views. All this is relevant to the justification for free speech that stems from distrust of government power (as mentioned in Chapter 1, pp. 8–9).

Furthermore, whereas in a democracy the legislation passed on hate speech is subject to mechanisms of oversight and accountability, much of the regulation of hate speech is made by private actors on grounds that are hard for citizens to discover, investigate, and hence call to account. For example, Facebook uses complex algorithms, known only to itself, as well as an army of its own censors in order to take down what it deems to be hateful messages; and it has been accused of racial bias in doing so, for example in relation to the Black Lives Matter movement. Facebook is arguably the world's largest censor, deleting about 288,000 posts every month (Strossen 2018, p. 32).

Nonetheless hate speech regulation may be effective if it includes some democratic oversight and is the least restrictive alternative by comparison to any other measure. So-called time, place and manner restrictions enable hate speakers to convey their essential message, albeit in a more constrained and less inflammatory way (Brown 2015, pp. 38–9). For example, members of the Westboro Baptist Church – who believe that US military deaths are God's punishment for the admission of gay and lesbian service personnel in the US armed forces (and, more generally, for the United States' toleration of homosexuality) – are allowed to picket sites of military funerals only from a set distance during certain hours (*Phelps-Roper v Strickland* 2008; Strossen 2018, p. 57). This may be better than censorship, which embitters angry hate speakers even further and gives them the oxygen of publicity.

If one is not convinced that it is possible to draft fair and just hate speech legislation that can be impartially enforced, what are the alternatives? Should victims try to develop a thicker skin and not let hate speech infiltrate their self-conception? Several free speech scholars have advocated the alternative response of counterspeech, whereby the victims themselves or other citizens talk back to the hatemongers, describing their hurt, asserting their rights, and reaffirming their commitment to liberal values such as dignity and equality. Counterspeech may be direct, as when hate speech's victims engage with hate speakers, for example by disrupting a far-right rally or by approaching hate speakers in a shared institutional context – a workplace or a university. By contrast, indirect counterspeech consists of marches, meetings, demonstrations, and rejections and rebuttals of any hateful expression in social media and elsewhere online; it champions dignity and other liberal values without engaging bilaterally with hate speakers. Counterspeech (especially of the direct kind) is certainly burdensome for those prepared to employ it. It requires overcoming the distress or fearfulness that hate speech often induces, standing up for one's rights, clarifying one's objections in ways that others cannot bend or twist, and articulating an appropriate response, very often in a public setting where counterspeakers may enjoy little social authority. But counterspeech also offers considerable individual benefits to those prepared to engage in it: increased self-respect and respect from others; a greater sense of individual agency, efficacy, confidence and empowerment; and increased authority in future social interactions. Citizens who are not themselves targeted by hate speech can speak back to it too, expressing solidarity with its victims and recognising their plight. Corey Brettschneider (2012), for example, defends what he calls 'value democracy', where the state would fund and support associations such as civil rights groups and other NGOs that engage in counterspeech and where elected officials themselves would call out hate speech, publicly reaffirming the state's commitment to rights and dignity for all.

It is important, however, to be aware of some limitations of the counterspeech approach. To begin with, there seems to be something slightly perverse in extolling the benefits of counterspeech – such as greater self-respect and augmented political participation – when those benefits arise only because of the original injustice of hate speech (cf. Brown 2015, p. 260). Furthermore, addressing hate speakers directly is sometimes impossible, for example when hate speech consists of graffiti or anonymous online messages, or is practically unfeasible in the light of disparities in resources: for example, if a star newspaper journalist engages in hate speech, it is not very likely that members of a vulnerable group who are her targets will enjoy the opportunity to engage in counterspeech of equal prominence, at least not on the same platform (cf. Brown 2015, p. 261). Thus in 2015, when the British columnist Katie Hopkins described immigrants as 'cockroaches' and 'feral humans'[9] in the *Sun*, she was widely condemned, but the *Sun* did not report this counterspeech.

Even when counterspeech is feasible, and even if the victims of hate speech can find the courage to speak back, they may reasonably ask why they should face this dual burden. Moreover, vulnerable minorities are not much heard in public discourse – they suffer from what Fricker (2007) calls 'testimonial injustice'; but then their counterspeech alone will not do much to shift the social climate of hate. More generally, in view of the disparate kinds of harms that hate speech causes – assaults on dignity, stigma, degradation, discrimination, marginalisation, and so on – it is far from clear that counterspeech, even if successfully carried out, will do much to cancel or ameliorate them.

Perhaps, then, counterspeech is best considered a part of the toolkit of responses to hate speech, alongside hate speech laws, other regulations, educational programmes aimed at reducing hatred and prejudice within society, and measures designed to address the root injustices in employment, education, treatment by the police and so on that minorities suffer. If context matters in the world of hate speech, this applies to determining potential remedies just as much as it does to analysing the phenomenon itself.

Finally, what about the regulation of online hate speech, as a specific phenomenon? Most of our discussion in this chapter applies to both offline and online hate speech. However, the distinctive feature of online hate speech by comparison to its offline counterpart is its instantaneousness: 'the Internet encourages forms of hate speech that are spontaneous in the sense of being instant responses, gut reactions, unconsidered judgments, off-the-cuff remarks, unfiltered commentary, and first thoughts' (Brown 2018, p. 304). This, for Brown, has two key implications. First, the regulation of online hate speech is better carried out by Internet service providers (ISPs) than by the state, since the former possess the technological tools that enable them to respond quickly and effectively to instances of hate speech. Second, since the regulation of online hate speech normally happens retroactively (an ISP detects an instance of online hate speech in a blog, a website, etc. and only then removes it), there is always a chance that some people accessed that content before it was removed and circulated it more widely. This, Brown concludes, renders the regulation of online hate speech less morally problematic than censorship *ex ante* (literally 'from before' [publication]), which was normal practice with offline hate speech in traditional media – although we should point out that it is also less effective.

Sadly, hate speech is likely to be with us for good; and, besides the normative issues surrounding its regulation, the practical means by which that regulation is effected will increasingly need to attend to its online forms.

3
Holocaust Denial

Introduction

Across the western world anti-Semitism is on the rise. While Jewish people have been victims of hatred and violence throughout the centuries, the recent rise of far-right extremism in the United States, Europe and elsewhere has resulted in a significant increase in the number of racially motivated attacks against them. This chapter does not examine anti-Semitism per se. We focus instead on a specific aspect of it that has been central to debates on free speech for some time: Holocaust denial.

The Holocaust is one of the most horrendous atrocities committed in the history of humankind. During the Second World War, 6 million Jews were killed by the German Nazi regime, especially through the extensive use of gas chambers in extermination camps across central Europe. Other victims of the Nazi regime were Roma, ethnic Poles and other Slavs, Soviet POWs, communists, homosexuals, Jehovah's Witnesses, and mentally and physically disabled people. The word 'holocaust' comes from the ancient Greek *holokaustos* (ὁλόκαυστος 'completely burnt', a compound of ὅλως 'entirely' < ὅλος 'whole' and καυστός 'burnt' < καίω 'kindle'). The Holocaust is also often referred to as the Shoah, from the Hebrew HaShoah (האושה 'the catastrophe').

So what is Holocaust denial? On a literal definition, Holocaust deniers are simply those who deny one or more of the historical truths about the Holocaust (the fact that there was a systematic extermination of around 6 million Jews, that this was carried out by using gas chambers, etc.). This seems indeed necessary, but not sufficient, for a satisfactory definition of the term. On our view, to qualify as a Holocaust denier, someone must *both* make false or inaccurate claims about the Holocaust *and* have some anti-Semitic intention. We emphasise the latter condition, since there is the possibility that serious historical research may legitimately challenge some aspects of the Holocaust. For example, there is a long-standing historiographical debate between so-called 'intentionalists', who argue that the Holocaust was mainly the result of a master plan devised by Adolf Hitler, and 'functionalists', for whom there was no such plan and who claim that two of the key factors that led to the Holocaust were Germany's economic situation and the way in which political power was arranged within the Nazi regime (Mason 1981). We do not think that functionalists should be labelled Holocaust deniers. To be considered that, a person must also aim to advance an anti-Semitic agenda, for example by claiming that the Holocaust or some of its basic facts did not happen and were just a fabrication designed to support the creation of a Jewish state (cf. Teachout 2006, p. 663) – which implies that Jewish people are evil and deceptive. It is this kind of anti-Semitic attitude, rather than genuine historical research, that leads Holocaust deniers to adopt a selective or distorted approach to historical evidence.

A UK poll from 2019, for example, found that about 5 per cent of British people believed that the Holocaust was a myth and a further 8 per cent believed that estimates of the number of people killed have been exaggerated.[1] Furthermore, even when people do not explicitly deny the Holocaust, they may be ignorant about it. In a 2018 poll conducted across Europe a third of respondents reported that they knew little or nothing about the Holocaust and 5 per cent said that they had never heard of it.[2] In the United States, a recent survey revealed that '[a]lmost a quarter of respondents (23%) ... believed the Holocaust was a myth, or had been exaggerated, or they weren't sure'; moreover, '63% of respondents did not know 6 million Jews were murdered during the Holocaust, and more than one in three (36%) thought 2 million or fewer had been killed'.[3] These figures may be due to ignorance, lack of interest, confusion, latent anti-Semitism or some combination of these factors, as well as exposure to online or print media that cast doubt on the Holocaust. While not all these claims are instances of Holocaust denial per se, they should still concern us. When deniers target audiences whose knowledge of the facts of the Holocaust is poor, they will probably find it easier to persuade them than those in command of the facts.

That Holocaust denial is a pressing social problem, especially owing to its link with anti-Semitism, is confirmed by its growing online presence. In 2016, for example, the chatterbot 'Tay' released by Microsoft on Twitter soon began 'a crash-course in racism, Holocaust denial and sexism',[4] saying things such as: 'Repeat after me, Hitler did nothing wrong.'[5] As a result, Tay was taken offline by Microsoft. In 2020 an investigation carried out by the UK-based Institute for Strategic Dialogue found that Facebook's search algorithm actively promoted denialist pages and groups (and similar content was readily accessible on Twitter, Reddit and YouTube).[6] Facebook defended such activities as a means to protect legitimate historical debate; but what it framed in this way in fact enabled anti-Semites to delegitimise Jewish suffering and to perpetuate long-standing anti-Semitic tropes.[7] In late 2020, in the light of growing anti-Semitism and ignorance about the Holocaust, especially among young people, Facebook finally reversed its policy.[8] These examples show that Holocaust denial is not a thing of the past but a still pervasive phenomenon, especially as a result of social media's capacity to amplify falsehoods rapidly. Nor is Holocaust denial merely an online phenomenon these days. In the summer of 2020, vandals scrawled denialist graffiti on a wall in the village that had been the site of the Nazis' biggest massacre of civilians in France.[9]

Several countries across Europe, as well as Israel, have had Holocaust denial laws for some time. These include Austria, Belgium, the Czech Republic, France, Germany, Hungary, the Netherlands, Poland, Portugal, Romania, Slovakia, Spain and Switzerland. Holocaust denial was also among the 'crimes of genocide' targeted by the 'Framework Decision on Combating Racism and Xenophobia' (Council of the European Union 2007). The United Kingdom does not have a Holocaust denial law, though this has not prevented the prosecution of individuals who have denied it on the grounds that they committed another criminal offence.[10] The United States does not and, unless it radically changed its legal traditions, could not have a Holocaust denial law. Such a law would violate the First Amendment and its cardinal principle of viewpoint neutrality, according to which the government must never proscribe speech that expresses a particular message. Given the importance of that principle and the very different approaches states have taken, the issue of Holocaust denial presents an interesting case study of the appropriate limits of extremist speech.

While Holocaust denial is a widespread phenomenon, there are some key figures who have particularly contributed to it, such as Paul Rassinier (1975), Arthur Butz (1976), and writers who published their work in the US-based pseudo-academic *Journal for Historical Review*, which, under the guise of being an outlet for 'revisionist historians', provided a platform for Holocaust deniers from 1980 until its demise in 2002. But the most influential Holocaust denier is probably the British writer David Irving. His book *Hitler's War* (Irving 1977) denied key aspects of the Holocaust and downplayed Hitler's involvement in it. Irving became the target of the American historian Deborah Lipstadt's criticism. In her book *Denying the Holocaust*, Lipstadt argued that

> Irving is one of the most dangerous spokespersons for Holocaust denial. Familiar with historical evidence, he bends it until it conforms with his ideological leanings and political agenda ... demands 'absolute documentary proof' when it comes to proving the Germans guilty, but ... relies on highly circumstantial evidence to condemn the Allies. (Lipstadt 1994, p. 181)

Because of these accusations, Irving sued Lipstadt and her publisher, Penguin Books, for libel in the United Kingdom. Given the way libel laws work in the United Kingdom as opposed to the United States, Lipstadt had to prove that

Irving was a Holocaust denier (rather than Irving having to prove that he was not), and after a long and very public trial she and her legal team succeeded (*Irving v Penguin Books Limited* 2000). The trial was portrayed in the 2016 movie *Denial*.[11]

In the next section we will make some general comments on the wrongs of Holocaust denial, before going on to assess, through the lenses of the three overarching arguments for freedom of speech, on what grounds it may or may not be legally regulated.

Holocaust denial: Hate, harm and context

Given the association of Holocaust denial with anti-Semitism, an obvious question to ask is whether it is a kind of hate speech. This is indeed how Holocaust denial is treated by some writers (e.g. Cohen-Almagor 2008; Brown 2015, pp. 29–30); and our definition of it as motivated by anti-Semitism would also fit in with the generic view of hate speech as an attack on the civic standing of its targets, as we described it in Chapter 2. Given the central role that the memory of the Holocaust plays in contemporary Jewish identity, it seems hard to avoid the conclusion that Holocaust denial is a form of hate speech. It taps into the familiar anti-Semitic trope of devious Jews who manipulate others for their own ends, for example by marshalling support for the establishment of the state of Israel after the Second World War or seeking to gain society's sympathy more generally. But if Holocaust denial is a form of hate speech, this raises a number of further questions. What precisely is the harm of denial, given the variety of harms associated with hate speech that we considered in the previous chapter? Does any country with existing laws against hate speech really need a separate Holocaust denial law? Is Holocaust denial more egregiously harmful in some contexts than others?

On the first question there are a few candidates. Holocaust denial might be regarded as an incitement to hatred, given its association with anti-Semitism and the continuing attacks on Jews and synagogues across the world. Incitement can be interpreted in a strict sense, like the 'imminent lawless action' principle in the United States (*Brandenburg v Ohio* 1969), but in the case of Holocaust denial it makes sense to think of it in a looser sense: it contributes to fuelling a climate of hatred against Jews, at least in some segments of the population (see Brown 2008). On this view, Holocaust denial laws are a means of preventing such hatred from spreading, though whether they are a necessary means is a further question. Holocaust denial might also be harmful because it defames Jews as a group in a way that damages their reputation; it asserts a falsehood about them; and it stereo-types them as liars and manipulators. It could also be seen as an affront to Jews' dignity, either simply as a reprehensible viewpoint, or because it casts doubt on their credentials as members in good standing of society. Either way, Holocaust denial laws could be seen as a way of symbolically affirming that dignity, an assertion bound up with the empirical truth that the Holocaust did indeed occur.

However, given that everyone in society has a right to dignity, a right not to be defamed and not to have hatred directed against her or him, this raises the second question, of whether any country really needs a separate Holocaust denial law alongside more general hate speech laws (where the latter exist). One could take the view that, although Holocaust denial, like other forms of hate speech, is wrong, there should be no law against it specifically, even if hate speech in general is regulated. In countries such as Germany, Austria and Israel, however, the memory of the Holocaust plays a key role in people's collective self-understanding, so laws against it in those places have a special valence or urgency.

But what about other states, which have been less affected by the Holocaust and yet have specific laws criminalising Holocaust denial? What makes the Holocaust and its denial special in those countries? One view is that the Holocaust was a uniquely evil event, perhaps because it sought to humiliate and eradicate an entire people, with no further political objective (Margalit and Motzkin 1996). But there have been other genocides in the twentieth century – in Armenia during the First World War, in Cambodia under the Khmer Rouge and, most recently, in Rwanda. Normally these are not the object of specific legal proscriptions, though an exception is France, where under the Gayssot Act (1990) it is illegal to question the existence of crimes against humanity.[12] Holocaust denial laws might also be defended on the pragmatic basis that existing hate speech laws, given the way they are interpreted in a particular state, may not effectively do the job of protecting Jews from the harm of denial.

On the third question – that of context – our focus in this chapter will be on Holocaust denial in the public sphere when deniers' statements, often amplified by social media, become known to a sizeable constituency. Whether Holocaust denial should be banned in private or secret meetings (e.g. of far-right groups) is a more contentious question. Another important context for denial is the academy, that is, universities, colleges and schools, as we shall briefly discuss.

Holocaust denial and truth

What do the three theories of free speech tell us about Holocaust denial and its regulation? The conceptual resources offered by the argument from truth are especially pertinent in this context. After all, Holocaust denial is the denial of a historical truth, one documented by countless historical sources, including official documents and eyewitnesses. So in what way can Mill's theory help us to establish whether Holocaust denial should be tolerated in a liberal democracy? In order to answer this question, it is worth returning to the specific arguments presented by Mill.

The first, to recall from Chapter 1 (see p. 12), is the infallibility argument, according to which silencing an opinion is wrong because that opinion may be true, and in that case silencing it would preserve error. Following this view, one could claim that we should not silence Holocaust denial, just in case it *may* be true. But the infallibility argument has broader implications. According to Mill, '[t]here must be discussion, to show how experience is to be interpreted. Wrong opinions and practices gradually yield to fact and argument: but facts and arguments, to produce any effect on the mind, must be brought before it' (Mill 2006, p. 27). Schauer explains Mill's point as follows:

We increase our knowledge by leaving our current opinions constantly open to revision, and in this way we justify acting on our current imperfect knowledge. Allowing the expression of that which we believe most fervently to be false thus gives us both the opportunity to increase our knowledge and the confidence that what we now believe imperfectly to be true is at least more likely true than any of the now-known alternatives. (Schauer 2012, p. 135)

Perhaps we should allow Holocaust denial, even if false, because freedom of speech will always cause wrong opinions to be gradually enfeebled and excluded from public debate. Eventually, then, belief in Holocaust denial will wither away. But is such trust justified? Perhaps not.

First of all, it is important to note that permitting Holocaust denial has significant non-epistemic costs, which include its contribution to reduced social harmony and to widespread anti-Semitism, as well as the resulting negative implications for Jewish people's safety, dignity and self-respect (Schauer 2012, p. 132). These costs seem especially salient if Holocaust denial is indeed a form of hate speech. We noted in Chapter 1 how, by prioritising truth, Mill's argument for free speech tends to neglect these kinds of social costs.

Beyond these non-epistemic costs, allowing Holocaust denial also has potential epistemic costs that are especially relevant to Mill's argument. Our faith in the ability of free speech to eradicate false views gradually seems to be simply misplaced. According to Schauer, for example, 'the expression of the falsity may increase the number of people who believe in the proposition despite its falsity, or who have greater confidence in the truth of a false proposition than they did prior to its frequent or prevalent expression' (Schauer 2012, p. 136). This process can be affected by such factors as the style and charisma of speakers, the predisposition of listeners, and the frequency with which false views are presented (p. 137). This is an empirical issue, but it seems very pertinent in today's online media world. The way in which many falsehoods and fake news are channelled by new media nowadays and become widely endorsed suggests that the evidence may be on Schauer's side (we examine fake news in Chapter 6). Further, many of the people who look for conspiracy theory and far-right websites that host anti-Semitic opinions, including Holocaust denial, are not disinterested seekers of the truth, but individuals seeking confirmation for their latently anti-Semitic views. Allowing Holocaust denial, one might argue, will not weaken these wrong opinions but rather contribute to reinforcing them and moving them further away from the truth.

Mill's second argument is that by silencing an opinion, even one that is definitely false, we risk holding our true opinion as a dead dogma, in an unthinking and inanimate way. Could one argue that Holocaust denial has, albeit perversely, some positive effect, if it helps us to understand the Holocaust better and forces us to (re-)examine the existing evidence about it? Nigel Warburton, for example, claims that the Irving trial prompted historians of the Holocaust to amass their evidence against Holocaust deniers in greater detail than they had done previously. 'The existence of an enemy in the field', he argues, 'was sufficient to focus and reinvigorate their search for more conclusive evidence about precisely how the Nazis set about systematic killing in the Holocaust' (Warburton 2009, p. 34). Likewise, in a speech at Columbia University in 2007, Mahmoud Ahmadinejad, the former president of Iran, argued that historians should continue to research this historical event, as new findings always emerge in all fields of inquiry, including in the natural sciences, and therefore it is a mistake ever to consider the research process concluded.[13] (Given Iran's association with Holocaust denial, it is likely that there was an element of bad faith in this assertion.)

However, this raises an important question. Is it really worth pursuing further research on issues that seem to be definitely settled? As Catriona McKinnon points out, allowing the mathematically incompetent to doubt established mathematical truths doesn't really promote progress, but impedes it by wasting time (McKinnon 2007, p. 15). Even Mill agreed that, when it comes to such disciplines as mathematics, truths are so obvious that there is perhaps no need for them to be constantly challenged in order for us to acquire a better understanding of them. So one might argue that allowing people to deny the Holocaust simply in order to engage with them and acquire a deeper understanding of this historical event would be a waste of time. But in his discussion of free speech Mill also makes a distinction between mathematics and what we call the humanities and social sciences – disciplines that include history. In these, he argues, the key strength in an argument is always its ability to win out over alternative arguments. This seems to support the view that Holocaust denial should be allowed, although here we have to be careful.

Perhaps, in line with the dead dogma argument, allowing Holocaust denial might stimulate research on the debate we mentioned between 'intentionalists' and 'functionalists' and on similar topics in areas where there is genuine disagreement among legitimate historians. And perhaps this conclusion might also be supported by Mill's partial truth argument: different perspectives may provide us with a better understanding of the Holocaust overall. However, the existence of the Holocaust, its nature and scale, and the facts about it are settled and uncontroversial. When *these* basics are contested, Holocaust denial seems unlikely to offer the sort of alternative argument or perspective that would help us to acquire a better and deeper understanding of the truth if we were to engage with it. Furthermore, while Mill's partial truth argument applies to debates about the Holocaust when it comes to legitimate historical positions (e.g. both 'intentionalists' and 'functionalists' can give us useful insights into the history and causes of the Holocaust), it does not apply to the denial of basic facts about the Holocaust.

Holocaust denial and autonomy

As we saw in Chapter 1, there are different versions of the autonomy argument for free speech. Baker, for example, places great emphasis on the value of autonomous self-expression as a dimension of self-realisation. Dworkin argues that autonomous persons should not have their speech restricted merely because their fellow citizens think their views to be worthless or reprehensible. Both of these arguments have an obvious blind spot when it comes to Holocaust denial; they do not consider the costs – including the costs to autonomy – for third parties, in this case Jews. Again, this seems especially relevant if Holocaust denial is a form of hate speech. Further, with Baker's argument, it is not intuitively obvious that expressing clear falsehoods that are damaging to others contributes to a person's self-realisation. If the right to engage in Holocaust denial is to be defended via the notion of autonomy, then it needs to say something about these two issues.

A version of the argument from autonomy more promising for our purposes is Scanlon's listener-centred view: to recall, according to this view we are sovereign over our beliefs and over the way we act on them. Thus the state and other agents lack the authority to limit which views we encounter. This would seem to justify allowing Holocaust denial, even if doing so results in our believing the denial, embracing anti-Semitic views, and possibly even carrying out anti-Semitic acts. Although the latter are harmful, on Scanlon's view responsibility for such acts cannot be placed at the door of the speaker who communicates the false view. The autonomous person herself decides what to believe and how to act.

We saw in Chapter 1, however, that later on Scanlon revised his view significantly. He came to see that a plausible view of free speech regulation depended on the interests of bystanders, alongside those of the audience and those of the speakers themselves. This opens the way for restrictions on speech that are designed to protect the interests of anyone harmed by Holocaust denial. Scanlon also came to acknowledge that some forms of speech can bypass, or even subvert, our capacity for rational thinking, rather than respecting it. Although he does not use the example of Holocaust denial, it is not difficult to see that its false and pernicious nature is a reason to curtail it; after all, we cannot think rationally about an issue if we are not provided with the true facts. Other writers have taken that thought and applied it to the contemporary case of online denial, for example on far-right or other anti-Semitic websites. According to Alexander Brown,

> it should not be overlooked that people responsible for Holocaust denial websites might exert an undue influence over users, even users who choose to enter these sites. For

those responsible for these sites could be undermining the integrity of users' mental processes by exploiting false statements of fact or misleading presentations of evidence, or could be circumventing cognitive channels of persuasion by taking advantage of users' emotional need to feel part of a group. (Brown 2015, p. 120)

This would seem to justify some kind of state intervention to tackle Holocaust denial. But what kind of intervention? Brown suggests that states should compel the owners and designers of Holocaust denial websites 'to place in prominent positions links to other websites detailing all of the available evidence supporting the existence of the Holocaust, or forcing them to declare whenever they have partially selected, edited, or omitted evidence' (Brown 2015, p. 120). Yet Brown also points out that most online Holocaust deniers inhabit 'deliberative conclaves' where they exchange information exclusively with other deniers, so the effect of such a reform may be limited. It is possible that this is becoming less true, however, as in the example of Facebook's algorithm we mentioned earlier that promotes denialist material. So, even if there are substantial practical issues involved in enforcing changes to websites, such online regulation might prompt curious individuals who are ignorant about the Holocaust to look beyond denialist propaganda.

Although most Holocaust denial these days is probably expressed online, in the context of the autonomy argument in particular it is also important to consider the substantially offline environment of education, since it is via schools and colleges that many young people will first acquire knowledge of the Holocaust; and they will do so when their capacity for intellectual autonomy is not yet fully formed. Further, a number of high-profile instances of Holocaust denial have specifically occurred in educational establishments. For example, James Keegstra, a teacher in a state school in Eckville, Alberta, Canada, was dismissed in 1982 for teaching Holocaust denial to his 14–18-year-old students. In a pre-Internet environment, those students had fewer means of access to alternative information, and in a small Canadian town there was probably no Jewish population of any size that might have provided a counternarrative.

Keegstra told his students that Jews were 'child killers' who had created the Holocaust in order to gain sympathy (Garton Ash 2016, p. 232). As Raphael Cohen-Almagor says, Keegstra 'did not want rational critics. He wanted parrots' (Cohen-Almagor 2008, p. 224). Keegstra was accused of indoctrinating students and, in a judgement upheld by the Supreme Court of Canada later, in 1984, was convicted of wilfully promoting hatred.

In a similar case, between 1976 and 1991, Malcolm Ross, a schoolteacher in New Brunswick, Canada, was the target of a number of warnings and reprimands because he was known to defend Holocaust denial outside the school. In 1988 a parent filed a complaint with the Human Rights Commission. This resulted in Ross's dismissal, which was confirmed by a Supreme Court of Canada ruling in 1996. The Court ruled that Ross's conduct 'poisoned' the educational environment, given that his actions were widely known and that schoolteachers enjoy authority and trust in their relations with students (*Ross v New Brunswick School District No 15* 1996). Ross's case highlights our earlier point that the wrongness of Holocaust denial depends to some degree on context.

Along similar lines, McKinnon (2007) argues that there is no place for Holocaust deniers in the academy, say, in a university's history department, since any such denier would fail to meet the minimum standards of impartiality and responsiveness to evidence that characterise the professional historian. Ross's case also illustrates that the boundary between an on-duty and an off-duty expression of Holocaust denial can often get blurred in educational contexts. Suppose for example that a science professor contributed to Holocaust denial websites in his or her spare time. Should such a person be censured? Should people lose their job because they are Holocaust deniers, or racists, or homophobes and so on, if they do not express their views at work? Those questions raise issues of sincerity and trust, virtues especially appropriate, perhaps, in the public political sphere. We now turn to consider the matter of Holocaust denial in that context.

Holocaust denial and democracy

One version of the democratic argument for free speech is recipient-centred. It says that citizens require access to a full range of politically relevant information in order to make up their minds on political questions and contribute to democratic debate as informed individuals. It is difficult to see, however, why it would be necessary for citizens to learn the details of Holocaust denial – as opposed to knowing of the existence of such a viewpoint – in order to be effective democratic participants. On the contrary, the reverse position seems more plausible: citizens should be informed of the true facts of the Holocaust, for example in case there was public discussion about memory laws, or in case citizens were considering whether a politician who had expressed anti-Semitic views should be censured. True, this does not exactly imply that Holocaust denial should be legally banned. It does show, however, that there would be nothing especially anti-democratic about banning it, if regulation is to be aimed at improving the quality of information available to the public for democratic deliberation. On this version of the democratic argument, such a ban would not be an unjust abridgement of free speech.

The more common version of the democratic free speech argument hinges on the special importance of political speech and on citizens' right to engage in it. Citizens need to be able to express their politically relevant views freely when participating in political discussion or deliberating with one another about whom to vote for in democratic elections. The question is whether Holocaust denial is one such view. Perhaps it is. Holocaust denial is generally embedded in a larger political message that, even if anti-Semitic in tone, also concerns issues such as a country's historical consciousness and self-understanding (for example, how far its citizens were complicit in Nazi war crimes). As Eric Barendt writes, 'it may sometimes be difficult to disentangle the making of a false historical claim, such as Holocaust denial, from contro-versial political arguments with which it may be associated and which are entitled to free speech protection, despite their unpalatable and distasteful character' (Barendt 2005, p. 176).

Other things being equal, in political debate citizens must be permitted to voice and hear controversial views. If Holocaust denial is one component in a group's political message and the component cannot be detached from the broader message, then perhaps it should be permitted on democratic grounds. This is not simply abstract speculation. At the 2009 UN anti-racism conference, Iran's former president, Ahmadinejad, described Israel as 'a totally racist government' and argued that it had been created 'under the pretext of Jewish suffering', thus revealing the close connection between his own anti-Semitic and anti-Israeli views and his position on the Holocaust.[14] If we value the importance of unconstrained political debate, as defenders of the democracy argument normally do, then perhaps Ahmadinejad should be allowed to invoke Holocaust denial views as part of his political message.

A similar kind of conclusion was reached by the Supreme Court of Canada in the landmark case *R v Zundel* (1992). Ernst Zündel, a German-born anti-Semite who had settled in Canada, had been involved in the production of neo-Nazi material for many years and was convicted under Section 181 of the Canadian Criminal Code, which prohibits the intentional publication of false statements. But in 1992 the Supreme Court overturned Zündel's previous conviction. The new decision contained the following statement:

> Exaggeration – even clear falsification – may arguably serve useful social purposes linked to the values underlying freedom of expression. A person fighting cruelty against animals may knowingly cite false statistics in pursuit of his or her beliefs and with the purpose of communicating a more fundamental message, e.g., 'cruelty to animals is increasing and must be stopped' ... All of this expression arguably has intrinsic value in fostering political participation and individual self-fulfilment. (*R v Zundel* 1992)

As we saw in the chapter on hate speech, however, the problem with this line of argument is that it implausibly assumes that Holocaust denial leaves all participants in democratic debate unaffected. But because of its association with anti-Semitic views, Holocaust denial is likely to contribute to at least some of the harms of hate speech, as we suggested above. If, for example, it creates a climate of hatred in which Jews feel insecure or intimidated in public places, this climate will prevent them from participating in political debate, thus undermining the very rationale for free speech under the democracy argument. Of course, Holocaust denial might have the opposite effect, galvanising Jews to participate in public debate more actively than ever. Some Holocaust survivors and other Jews urged Facebook to remove posts that denied the genocide perpetrated by the Nazis (this was just before Facebook's change of policy; see p. 57).[15] But the affront to dignity that this act involves also seems inconsistent with the basic respect that all citizens should extend to one another in a democratic society.

Taken together, the Keegstra, Ross and Zündel cases – all, coincidentally, from Canada – illustrate a couple of general points about free speech and Holocaust denial. One is that, even though Canada does not have a specific Holocaust denial law, it is certainly still possible for it to punish deniers. And, obviously, this applies to other countries without specific legislation concerning Holocaust denial. In the United Kingdom, for example, Alison Chabloz was convicted in 2018 of using a public communications network to send offensive, indecent or menacing messages or material after she had posted online a number of songs, including one that called Auschwitz a 'theme park'.[16] Thus whether a country has any need to adopt a Holocaust denial law depends in part on whether its other free speech laws can be used effectively to prosecute denial. It could be argued that, when a state specifically outlaws Holocaust denial, this step affirms the dignity and political membership of Jews within its borders and elsewhere. But, as we said, such an action in turn raises the question of whether the denial of other genocides should be made illegal as well. From a legal perspective, a practical reason for singling out Holocaust denial could be that the Jewish diaspora is dispersed quite widely across the world: this fact makes the harm of Holocaust denial relevant to a broader range of countries than the harm of denial in the case of other genocides. However, genocides such as those committed in Armenia and Cambodia also targeted groups that are widely present across the world today.

As Keegstra and Ross were schoolteachers, these two cases raise the question of the best means of combating denial among young people. Both were dismissed from their posts, in Ross's case even though he did not broadcast his denialist views in the classroom. But laws and regulations governing employment and the like are blunt instruments; they can be used to remove teachers or lecturers only after the damage has been done (cf. Cohen-Almagor 2008). In educational settings, young people's opinions are still being shaped and their capacity for intellectual autonomy is still being formed. It therefore seems appropriate to focus on school curricula too, and on teaching materials, both print and online, to ensure that students receive an accurate view of the Holocaust and are able to ask critical questions about it as a significant episode in recent history. If this is not possible, young people could at least be taught about the sinister presence of far-right websites before they can be beguiled by them. If individuals are provided with comprehensive information about the Holocaust from childhood, so that they are able to evaluate deniers' claims critically, this will reduce the latter's ability to influence them. With adults, the situation is more difficult because, if a person wants to seek out anti-Semitic material or to become involved in a far-right movement, he or she surely will. Events such as Holocaust Memorial Day, or the occasional TV documentary or museum exhibition no doubt have some influence when it comes to educating the wider public. But their audiences are likely to be made up of people who already possess some basic knowledge of the Holocaust, not of denialist sympathisers. Holocaust denial laws will not make the speech they target go away any more than hate speech laws would. Even so, for the reasons we have indicated, they seem to be justified.

4

Offensive Speech

Introduction

A well-known novelist's book criticises the Prophet Muhammad, incensing millions of Muslims across the world; a play uses a Sikh temple as a setting for rape and murder; a poem describes Jesus having sex with Roman men. In this chapter we turn to speech and other expressive conduct that offends people, especially with regard to their religious or moral convictions.

It is commonly held that offensive speech is a less serious kind of harm than hate speech, if it even is a harm; and, while there is a good deal of truth in that view, if interpreted too literally it risks overlooking what is distinctive about offensive speech as a particular category. Hate speech, we said in Chapter 2, is best characterised as an assault on those it targets; more specifically, it attacks their status as equal members of the political community. To complicate matters, it is invariably offensive. Offensive (but not hate) speech is a slight or an affront to those who experience it, a mode of expression that does not show proper regard for them as belief holders. It need not undermine their civic status, though it may come very close to doing so.

This brief definition of offensive speech becomes clearer when we distinguish between three forms of offensive expression (Jones 2011, pp. 80–4). First, there is what we might call *moral* offence, a form distinguished by the fact that the offending party fails adequately to respect the moral or religious beliefs of those who are offended; she traduces or ridicules them, or insults their nature. Moral offence is the most important category of offensive expression. It covers all three examples with which we opened the chapter; and it is the kind that is hardest to distinguish from hate speech. However, people can be much exercised by a second, *conventional* kind of offence, which shares the basic form of moral offence in that it operates on people's beliefs, but differs from it insofar as those beliefs do not generally concern moral or religious questions. Conventional offence occurs when offending individuals fail to observe certain social codes, norms or customs. Appearing naked in public would be offensive in most places;[1] public displays of affection between two members of the same sex are offensive in some societies, as burning the national flag is in others.[2] Both moral and conventional offences may concern conduct other than speech. Finally, the third category, which can be termed *raw* offence, typically does not feature speech at all. Also, unlike the former two categories, it does not operate via people's beliefs, at least not in any straightforward way. Raw offence includes loud noises, unpleasant smells, unwelcome sights and other nuisances. These interrupt our normal activity as unwelcome distractions.

Our main focus in this chapter is on moral and conventional offence, since this variety raises the most acute issues in relation to freedom of speech. Unlike raw offence, which is direct or non-mediated, moral and conventional offences are mediated by and take effect only in the presence of certain norms or values, whether moral, cultural or social. This is significant for a number of reasons. First, it helps to clarify the analytic distinction between hate speech and offensive speech: the fact that some agent has violated a norm one holds dear does not by itself imply that the violation is an assault against one's status. If a person says 'forcing women to cover their faces is contemptible', that may be offensive, but it is not hate speech, whereas to say 'Muslims are contemptible' is hate speech (this is not a statement about what Muslims believe). When, before he became United

Kingdom's prime minister, Boris Johnson wrote in 2018 that Muslim women who wear the burka 'look like letter boxes',[3] that was certainly offensive – and possibly hate speech, too, if it communicated that these Muslim women are not proper members of the political community.[4] While there is some intuitive line between hate speech and offensive speech, it is not an easy one to draw.

Second, the reference to shared norms calls attention to the fact that, in much offensive conduct, the expressive dimension is non-verbal in nature, as the examples of flag burning and public nudity show. Finally, the fact that moral and conventional offences operate through the mediation of people's beliefs means that there are in principle two ways of reducing the incidence of the sort of conduct that offends these people: one is to regulate that sort of conduct, the other to encourage the people in question to change their beliefs. The latter does not apply in the case of hate speech: a person cannot evade the hateful force of a statement such as 'Muslims are contemptible' merely by abandoning Islam. However, while beliefs do not respond directly to one's will, they can and do change over time, for reasons that it is possible to influence through political reform. For example, not too long ago people would have been aghast at the sight of people of the same sex or of different races showing affection in public, but nowadays that attitude has changed, as most cultures live in more enlightened times.

Whether it is reasonable or feasible to ask people to work on their beliefs is a further question, and much depends on the type of beliefs at stake. It may be reasonable to ask racists or homophobes to work on their hostile beliefs, but it is not reasonable to ask Christians or Muslims to abandon their religious ones. Even so, the fact that it is possible for people to do so puts some distance – again – between offensive speech and hateful speech, since the latter targets characteristics that define people's identities, such as their race or ethnicity, and that cannot normally be changed or abandoned. Complications arise because religion is often a marker of ethnicity or place of origin, as it is for Muslims from South Asia or the Middle East. It may also be inherited; thus non-believing Jews are victims of anti-Semitic hate speech no less than religious Jews, since being Jewish is a matter of culture and matrilineal descent. But, just because there is no clear, bright line between hateful speech and offensive speech, it does not follow that there is no distinction to be drawn. Although hate speech is offensive, its wrong-making quality does not reside in its offensiveness – as we saw earlier. Whether the harm of offensive speech (where there is harm) is of a piece with the harm of hate speech, and when and how offensive speech should be regulated (if at all), are questions we keep in mind throughout the present chapter.

From blasphemy to offence

From 1676, when John Taylor was tried and convicted for stating that Jesus Christ was a 'whoremaster' and 'religion was a cheat', until eventual abolition in 2008, English law recognised a common-law offence of blasphemy, which until the eighteenth century tended to be equated with the crime of sedition (Jones 1980, p. 131). By the end of the twentieth century, however, prosecutions for blasphemy in England had all but dried up. The last successful prosecution was instigated by the conservative social activist Mary Whitehouse against the newspaper *Gay News* and its editor, Denis Lemon, in 1977. *Gay News* had published a poem by James Kirkup, 'The Love That Dare Not Speak Its Name', which depicted Christ having numerous sexual liaisons with Roman men, including Pontius Pilate. Lemon was found guilty and fined, narrowly escaping a prison sentence. He appealed to the House of Lords (the forerunner of the Supreme Court in England) but lost, and Lord Scarman opined that blasphemy law applied to those 'words' that 'cause grave offence to the religious feelings of some of their fellow citizens or are such as to tend to deprave and corrupt persons who are likely to read them' (*R v Lemon* 1979).

More recently, in 2007, the evangelical group Christian Voice attempted to bring a private prosecution for blasphemy against BBC's director general after the BBC had aired a TV adaptation of the hit show *Jerry Springer: The Opera*. This musical depicted God, Jesus, Mary, Adam and Eve, and Satan as warring guests on a special edition of the *Jerry Springer Show* and contained more than two hundred swear words. It was, according to Christian Voice, 'an offensive, spiteful, systematic mockery and wilful denigration of Christian belief'.[5] However, the group's attempt failed in the High Court.

Lord Scarman's comments on the *Gay News* case connect the prohibition of blasphemy to offence and its effect on persons, but for most of its history blasphemy law was understood rather as protecting religion itself. Thus, if people were offended by blasphemous depictions of Christ and his teachings, this is because those depictions attacked the sacred value of their religion. Indeed, states around the world that continue to have blasphemy laws invariably outlaw any vilification of the state religion rather than legislating against offences to people's religious feelings.

However, it is difficult to justify a blasphemy law that protects only Christianity – or any other religion, for that matter – in a multicultural context where different faiths coexist and must tolerate each other. Special protection for Christianity, but not for other faiths, could be defended only on the grounds that Christianity is uniquely correct; but this is not something on which a liberal state should take a stand. Indeed, the next time when debate on blasphemy erupted in the United Kingdom after the *Gay News* prosecution, it involved Islam. This happened after the publication, in 1988, of the well-known novelist Salman Rushdie's book *The Satanic Verses*. Rushdie's novel, written in his magic realist style, contained a dream sequence that depicts a thinly disguised version of the Prophet Muhammad – called Mahound or 'the messenger' – who renarrates passages from the Quran in favour of an old polytheistic religion and later states that this was a mistake induced by the devil. Soon after its publication, the novel attracted widespread criticism from many Muslims in Britain and across the world and stirred violent riots in Pakistan (where the book was banned) and elsewhere. In February 1989, Ayatollah Khomeini, the supreme leader of Iran, issued a fatwa that called for the death of Rushdie and his publishers. This fatwa remains in place today. Although Rushdie is still alive, a number of people have died as a result of the furore, including the Japanese translator of the book. An attempt by the British Muslim Action Front to commence legal proceedings against Rushdie on the basis of

England's blasphemy law failed, since the law protected only Christianity. This failure signals the obsoleteness of such laws in our increasingly religiously diverse societies.

If no religion is to enjoy any special position, the state in a multifaith society can level up so that all religions are protected from offensive speech, or level down so that none is. Levelling up is also a way of recognising that 'society is entitled to, or perhaps even should, protect a sense of the sacred ... Something valuable is lost if there are no restrictions at all on what can be said or written about God or religious belief' (Barendt 2005, p. 187). Extending blasphemy law to all faiths, however, would be to invite the state to determine what counts as a religion and the courts to decide what is sacred to each one. Moreover, from the perspective of the liberal doctrine of neutrality (Rawls 2005), protecting all religious beliefs from offence would still be a partisan position, as it would single them out against non-religious beliefs, which can be equally strong yet would remain unprotected.

Partly for these reasons, many liberal democracies have opted for a levelling down approach. In the United States, for example, even a blasphemy law protecting all faiths would be anathema to the First Amendment tradition, which separates between state and religion. England and Wales, too, adopted the levelling down approach soon after the Rushdie affair: in 2008 the common-law offence of blasphemy was abolished (it remains an offence in Scotland and Northern Ireland). The 2006 Racial and Religious Hatred Act was passed in response to the wave of Islamophobia that occurred in the wake of the 9/11 attacks in the United States and the 2005 terrorist bombings in London. This Act extended to religions the existing law on inciting racial hatred (Brown 2008); but it was accompanied by an important proviso. After a backlash led by prominent figures in the arts who claimed that the Act would stifle criticism of religion, a clause was inserted in the final version that explicitly stated that 'expressions of antipathy, dislike, ridicule, insult or abuse' of religion were legally permitted (Section 29J). Thus religion is not especially protected in Britain from offensive criticism – not any more than it is in the United States.

The concept of blasphemy depersonalises the notion of offence by focusing on attacks against beliefs and values that a society shares – if indeed it does; then it moralises them by assuming that those beliefs and values are correct. In a diverse society, where 'shared beliefs' often simply means majority beliefs, these two manoeuvres constrain freedom of speech. We need to refocus on norms and values as properties of individuals' commitments and recognise that these can change. To explore whether there is a case for the regulation of offensive speech from a liberal perspective, we turn once again to our three general theories of free speech. In the case of hate speech, we saw that none of these accounts gave unequivocal guidance on the question of regulation. Does the same apply to offensive speech?

Offensive speech and truth

Does offensive speech serve the truth in society? In Chapter 3 we noted how the expression of hatred may serve the valuable purpose of allowing the reasonable majority to contest its message by using rational argument, and thus may turn us towards the truth, at least in the long run. More than hate speech, offensive speech could contain a grain of truth. For artistic or political reasons, it seems to be important for some people to say or write things that, foreseeably if not intentionally, give offence. Satire and parody of people's religious or political views, for instance, typically contain a good dose of truth; they distort and exaggerate in order to make an underlying point. Even if they are offensive, or perhaps especially then, they may encourage their viewers to see a religion in a new light, perhaps to their own benefit as well as others'. Further, the experience of offensive speech can help to build up a person's psychic constitution even more than the experience of hate speech. Jeremy Waldron (1987), for example, claims that being forced to engage with views that one finds challenging and uncomfortable benefits individuals' intellectual and moral development – a position he attributes to Mill. Interpreted in this way, readiness to give and appropriately receive offence would be the mark of an enlightened, liberal society.

In general, then, the consequentialist argument from truth

seems to be quite permissive when it comes to the freedom to offend. But one should sound a note of caution that applies to the consequences of offensive speech independently of its truth-based defence. Offence, like hate, can escalate; indeed, it often does not take much for offensive speech to turn into hate speech. *Pace* Waldron's argument, a culture of offence might coarsen rather than refine our ethical sensibilities. Particularly when offence is directed against a vulnerable religious group, it may cause harm and render further offence (or even hate) more likely, as well as somewhat legitimate in the eyes of others. At the same time, however, this argument can be reversed. Robert Simpson (2018), for example, argues that laws and rules that proscribe offensive speech can serve as a sort of social licence for those who bear the brunt of such speech to feel offended, and thus have the counterproductive effect of *increasing* offence taking in society at large. Plainly, specific circumstances will determine to a substantial extent whether the offence-reduction or offence-escalation model takes effect.

Offensive speech and autonomy

In Chapter 2 we concluded that the autonomy argument's implications for hate speech were ambiguous. Does a similar conclusion apply in the case of offensive speech?

Clearly, if restrictions on free speech are an illegitimate intrusion on speakers' autonomy, then that will apply just as much to offensive as it does to hate speech. Indeed, while it might reasonably be argued that hate speakers should reformulate their basic message in non-hateful terms, in the case of offensive speech the doctrine that 'the manner is the message' is more plausible. George Sher (2020) has suggested that would-be offensive speakers are themselves offended if they are prohibited from expressing their views; if so, then avoiding offence is pitched against avoiding offence, just as considerations of autonomy lie on both sides of the hate speech debate. It is less clear, however, whether there is moral or even psychological parity between the offence that would-be speakers could suffer and the offence that they are likely to cause. What is certain is that parody, ridicule, satire and abuse of deeply held religious beliefs are inevitably going to offend some of the people who hold them. Yet take out these elements and the religious critic's message will be reduced to a bland commentary.

What the autonomy argument implies for offensive speech seems therefore to hinge on whether the expression of offensive material undermines, subverts, or otherwise disrespects the autonomy of those it is aimed at. To address this question, let us focus on one of the most prominent cases of allegedly blasphemous speech in recent times. On 30 September 2005, the centre-right Danish Newspaper *Jyllands-Posten* published twelve cartoons that lampooned Islam, most of them depicting the Prophet Muhammad. The cartoons were, according to the newspaper, an attempt to contribute to public debate about criticism of Islam and self-censorship. In one of them, Muhammad is drawn carrying a bomb in his turban. In another, he is portrayed outside the gates of heaven, imploring suicide bombers with the message 'stop, stop, we've run out of virgins'. Yet another depicts a boy named Muhammad in the process of writing on a blackboard, in Arabic letters, 'The editors of *Jyllands-Posten* are a bunch of reactionary provocateurs'. The *Jyllands-Posten* cartoons returned to the forefront of public debate in September 2020, when the French satirical newspaper *Charlie Hebdo* decided to republish them before the beginning of a trial of suspected accomplices of the terrorists who attacked its offices in January 2015.[6]

For Muslims in Denmark, and very soon for Muslims across the world, the cartoons were a double blow – first, because the material depiction of Muhammad is considered blasphemous in Islam and, second, because the cartoons themselves were deemed highly offensive. The publication of the cartoons sparked an immediate debate about the place of Islam and the limits of freedom of expression in Denmark. Soon there were demonstrations across the world. The Danish prime minister and his government took a hard line in defending the cartoons and refused to meet with Muslim representatives, thus exacerbating their anger. At the time, Denmark had a blasphemy law that made it a criminal offence to issue public utterances 'threatening, insulting or degrading to a group of persons' on various grounds, including their faith (Lægaard 2007, pp. 485–6). Yet the Danish public prosecutor judged that the cartoons did not infringe this law. Coming only a few years after the 9/11 attacks and the western military intervention in Afghanistan and Iraq, feelings were already inflamed, and some protests turned violent, yielding a significant number of deaths.

What can the *Jyllands-Posten* controversy teach us in the area of autonomy and offence? One conclusion is that the line between offence and hate is hard to draw. In our view, the cartoons were profoundly offensive, but they were not hate speech because they mocked Islam rather than expressing hatred towards Muslims themselves. Others may disagree.

According to Christian Rostbøll (2009), the problem with arguments advanced by some defenders of the newspaper was that they invoked a very controversial conception of individual autonomy. According to this 'Millian' conception (as Rostbøll labels it), to be autonomous means to be able and willing to engage in a process of constant critical self-reflection regarding one's beliefs. This implies that, when someone targets our religious beliefs via speech that we consider offensive or blasphemous, we should not try to silence them but rather take this as an opportunity to re-examine our beliefs critically. According to Rostbøll, this is an arrogant conception of autonomy, as it seeks to impose upon sincere religious adherents a particular way of living their faith, one that is very demanding and that many of them would reject, as would other citizens.

In its place, Rostbøll argues, we should embrace a 'Kantian' conception of autonomy, according to which respecting others as autonomous persons means respecting them as persons 'the realization of whose ends is as important as the realization of our own' (Rostbøll 2009, p. 633). We should assume that others, just like us, have endorsed or sanctioned their ends in a reflective manner, and therefore we should accord these a status equal to that of our own ends. Thus, contrary to the prime minister's decision, Danish Muslims should have been invited to participate in a public debate on the limits of speech. The Kantian conception of autonomy demands humility rather than arrogance. Yet Rostbøll's conclusion is not that the *Jyllands-Posten*'s cartoons should have been censored. He claims instead that, while it was appropriate to grant the newspaper a legal right to free speech, the editors and cartoonists had a moral duty of self-regulation, that is, a duty to censor themselves in order to respect in Kantian fashion the autonomy of Muslims. Rostbøll's argument is enlightening for several reasons. It shows, once again, the connection between autonomy-based and consequentialist arguments for free speech. The Millian conception of autonomy that he opposes is grounded in Mill's view that free speech should be used to promote individuals' critical and deliberative capacities. Relatedly, Rostbøll's argument highlights the way in which substantive autonomy is a controversial justification for free speech in diverse societies, as we mentioned in Chapter 1. His attempt to ground this freedom in a thinner Kantian conception of autonomy constitutes an important step towards providing a more publicly acceptable justification for it. Indeed his conception of Kantian autonomy resembles what John Rawls refers to as one of our 'moral powers', namely 'the capacity to form, to revise, and rationally to pursue a conception of one's rational advantage or good' (Rawls 2005, p. 19). A liberal state can recognise and promote every citizen's right to exercise this moral power in a way that is respectful of all its citizens' diverse conceptions of the good. Finally, Rostbøll's argument shows that legal regulation is not the only available response to wrongful speech. Alongside counterspeech, self-censorship (accompanied perhaps by social stigma) may sometimes be a suitable way of regulating certain kinds of speech without resorting to coercive law. Other possible policy responses are official retractions, fines, apologies and compensations, as well as the various ways in which contending parties might mediate their disagreement in civil society (Lægaard 2007, p. 484).

Offensive speech and democracy

Finally, what of the democratic argument for free speech? The general form of this argument is that public speech is a necessary part of a democratic political culture, which in turn is necessary if citizens are to debate issues in a democratic society. Put this way, the argument may appear quite sympathetic to offensive speech, at least if that kind of speech has some positive role by contributing to public debate (e.g. Post 2007). Even speech that ridicules certain religious beliefs may play a part, perhaps even a healthy part, by helping citizens to form views of the religion targeted. These views may be relevant to public debate in areas such as abortion, euthanasia, same-sex marriage and religious education. The offence that ridicule and satire cause among conscientious believers is the price to be paid for robust public debate; in a pluralistic society no group can expect its positions to be beyond criticism, and in diverse societies this criticism may be robust.

To be sure, one can reply to all this with a parallel form of the argument that we mentioned in our discussion of hate speech in Chapter 2: offensive expression can impede the public participation of members of those groups that find themselves at the receiving end of it. However, this depends on a variety of factors such as the degree to which a religious minority is marginalised or is more vocal than others in the public domain, and how far the messages it finds offensive are directed at its beliefs or at its members as individual believers. In the Danish cartoons controversy, it was the Danish Muslims who actively sought a meeting with the prime minister; and it was the prime minister who refused to discuss the issue with them. But if offensive messages ostensibly directed at a minority's religious beliefs are really a proxy for attacking that minority itself and its members qua members, then the resulting offence is very similar to targeted hate speech – and in that case the considerations we listed against the democratic argument in Chapter 2 apply.

While context does matter, in general it seems fair to conclude that the justifying arguments for free speech will give more latitude to offence than to hate – as we would expect, given that the former tends to cause less harm (when any at all).

Offensive nuisances, profound offences and Joel Feinberg's 'offence principle'

No discussion of offensive speech is complete unless it examines the contribution of Joel Feinberg in his magisterial four-volume *The Moral Limits of the Criminal Law*. Volume 2 of that work, *Offense to Others* (Feinberg 1985), examines in some detail the nature and meaning of offensive conduct. At its most general, Feinberg's view is that Mill's harm principle should be supplemented with an offence principle, the implication being that at least some offensive but not harmful conduct is of sufficient magnitude to justify official intervention. However, matters are fairly complex, because Feinberg introduces an intricate balancing test to determine when legal regulation is appropriate, and also because he distinguishes between offensive nuisances and profound offences; and, to judge by the main example he provides for the latter, it looks very much as if harm may be involved.

We will consider profound offences in a moment, but before doing that we need to introduce Feinberg's notion of offensive nuisances and explain the relevant factors in his balancing test. In fact Feinberg's category is a miscellany of experiences of different kinds: affronts to the senses, for example loud noises and bad smells; disgust and revulsion, for example at someone's eating habits; shocks to moral, religious or patriotic sensibilities, caused for example by flag desecration, or by a person's wearing a T-shirt that depicts Jesus on the cross with the message 'Hang in there baby!'; shame, embarrassment and anxiety, for example at public nudity or sex; annoyance and frustration, for example with the boring chatterer who sits next to you on public transport; and fear, resentment, humiliation and anger, caused for example by racist slogans in the vicinity (Feinberg 1985, pp. 10–13).

This is a diverse list, which cuts across our original distinction between non-mediated and mediated offences – and also, perhaps, between convention-based and moral offences within the latter category. Annoyance and frustration are irritations but, generally speaking, they are not experiences of offence. Conversely, not all these unwelcome experiences are most aptly characterised by the label 'nuisance'. Much depends on the hearer's background. Religiously offensive speech, for example, may be deeply and wrongfully offensive, not simply a nuisance, when those whose beliefs it targets belong to groups that suffer persistent social injustices such as marginalisation (Bonotti and Seglow 2019). Likewise, racist shouting could be quite threatening for members of certain minorities. And, of course, not all these offensive nuisances are instances of speech or expression.

The list of factors that, according to Feinberg (1985, pp. 30–5), bear upon the regulation of offensive conduct is also various. First, there is the intensity, durability and extent of the repugnance that offensive conduct provokes. Second, there is the ease with which a person can avoid offensive displays; for instance, the ability to avoid political rallies in support of causes that one finds offensive is usually a straight-forward matter. Third and relatedly, there is what Feinberg calls the *volenti* standard, which he extracts from the general principle that *volenti non fit iniuria* ('no harm is done to a willing/consenting participant') – that is, how far a person has willingly taken the risk of experiencing offensive conduct; for example, it is generally easy for someone to avoid viewing TV programmes or look at websites that may offend her.[7] Finally, Feinberg says, we must discount 'abnormal suscep-tibilities', as in the case of an oversensitive person who is disproportionately upset by loud noises or unwelcome sights.

These considerations are weighed against a number of factors that count in favour of freedom to offend through speech or conduct (Feinberg 1985, p. 44). First, actions that are of personal importance to the actor herself, or have social value more generally, enjoy greater immunity from regulation. As Feinberg notes, the noise from a demolition site might be an offensive nuisance, but it is generally accepted that new buildings need to be constructed. Likewise, a book that offends, such as *The Satanic Verses*, will have personal importance for its author and for some of its readers. What this first criterion rules out is offensive conduct that is frivolous, wanton, perverse or gratuitous, and not connected to anything in the speaker's or the public's genuine interest, such as noisy arguments from an apartment that disturb the neighbours. At the same time, some offensive behaviour is valuable for its perpetrator only *because* it is conducted in public, for example dressing in provocative clothes such as the Jesus T-shirt mentioned earlier.

A second factor is the availability of alternative times and places for the behaviour, such that it would cause less offence; thus a very loud rock concert might be held in a far-off field, not the middle of a city park. Another consideration is the extent, if any, to which offence is caused by spiteful or malicious motives: these should be generally discounted, just as frivolously caused offence is. Conversely, what Feinberg calls 'conscientious' offence involves the intention to communicate something that the speaker considers valuable. This is particularly likely in the case of artists and novelists, who often employ offensive material to convey a significant message. For example, when Gurpreet Kaur Bhatti's play *Behzti* (2004), which portrayed a Sikh temple as the setting for rape, physical abuse, and murder, was fiercely criticised by Britain's Sikh community, the playwright explained her artistic choice thus: 'I did not write *Behzti* to offend. It is a sincere piece of work in which I wanted to explore how human frailties can lead into a prison of hypocrisy' (Bhatti, cited in Warburton 2009, p. 54).

Finally, there is the question of whether the offensive conduct that takes place in some location is experienced there commonly or rarely. The thought seems to be that, if offensive conduct is common somewhere, then people will be inoculated against it to some extent. Although this may be true in some contexts, we have also drawn attention to the fact that repeated occurrences of an offence may wound through repetition. It is probable that Feinberg does not think that this applies in the case of offensive nuisances.

Feinberg's considerations seem sensible; yet it is noteworthy that he does not invoke a standard of reasonableness in evaluating behaviour that some people find offensive. According to this standard, speech or behaviour that recognizes the free and equal status of others is reasonable, whereas that which denies it is unreasonable (see e.g. Rawls 2005). Employing such a standard would mean that reasonable speech and expression that some people find offensive should be permitted, while unreasonable speech and offensive expression should not.

Feinberg rejects this approach. Thus, if city authorities allow a demonstration of liberal-minded citizens in support of migrants to go ahead but ban a far-right march against it, this will be not because one cause is reasonable and the other is not, but rather because of the sorts of factors we have just canvassed. (In this sense, Feinberg's approach is related to the doctrine of viewpoint neutrality in free speech.) The putative far-right demonstration might be judged to be spiteful or malicious, for instance, or perhaps larger, noisier or rowdier than the demonstration conducted by liberal citizens. The main reason why Feinberg objects to a reasonableness test is that, in his view, legislators do not have the prerogative of determining the reasonableness of citizens' emotional reactions to various forms of offensive conduct (Feinberg 1985, pp. 35–7). This, he says, would be 'dangerous and distinctly contrary to liberal principles' (p. 37) as well as redundant, given the other criteria he enumerates.

Although Feinberg's liberal intuition is a sound one, we can still enquire whether a reasonableness test might be appropriate. Here it is useful to identify the norms or values underlying individuals' attitudes of offence; and this is possible only if one makes the distinction between an offence mediated by beliefs and an unmediated offence in a way Feinberg does not. Thus one could distinguish between taking offence at conduct that respects individuals' free and equal status (e.g. two gay men kissing or holding hands), which is unreasonable, and taking offence at conduct that fails to respect those values (e.g. Nazis painting swastikas on a public wall), which is by that token reasonable (Shoemaker 2000). On this basis we can discount the offence taken by some people at the sight of same-sex or mixed-race couples, for example; or we can avoid treating a civil rights demonstration and a far-right political demonstration in the same way. To examine this point in more detail, we will consider a real example of a far-right march. But before doing so we need to mention the second of Feinberg's two major categories of offences.

Profound offences, explains Feinberg, are deep, shattering and serious. This category contains offences that are taken because an act is believed to be wrong (as opposed to being judged wrong because it offends, as in conventional

offence). The offence involved is impersonal and not necessarily related to one's status as a victim, as in our example of
liberal-minded citizens offended by a far-right rally (Feinberg
1985, pp. 57–60). Profound offences violate norms and
values rooted in our moral or religious convictions, or at the
very least deeply held conventions. Ruled out of the frame,
however, is what Feinberg (p. 60) calls 'bare knowledge'
offences, that is, situations where individuals are offended
by speech or conduct they do not witness at first hand. For
example, many Americans would be offended by reports
of US flags burning far from where they live, and many
Christians would be offended by *Jerry Springer: The Opera*
even without seeing it. Here again, Feinberg takes a distinctly
liberal line: mere knowledge that an event occurs cannot be a
setback to one's interests.

Feinberg's central example of profound offence is the
planned march of the National Socialist Party of America
through the town of Skokie, Illinois in 1977. At the time,
Skokie had a large Jewish population that included about
5,000–7,000 Holocaust survivors, and the purpose of the
American Nazi Party marching in full regalia was, as Feinberg
puts it, to 'insult them, lacerate their feelings and indirectly
threaten them' (p. 86). If anything is to qualify as profoundly
offensive, then this march is.

The case achieved notoriety after the American Civil
Liberties Union controversially declared that the Nazis should
be permitted to march, given their First Amendment rights
to free speech and assembly, and the US Supreme Court
concurred with this judgement. The decision struck down a
number of ordinances against the proposed march that the
Village of Skokie had passed after discussions conducted
among the local Jewish community. In the end the march
never took place owing to the high cost of insurance that the
town of Skokie imposed upon the Nazis, but the case remains
a notorious one in the annals of free speech.

It is a natural response to regard the Skokie march as an
instance of hate speech, and indeed Feinberg himself says
that it was 'very close to the pure insult extreme' (p. 86).
In that context, Feinberg's view that the march should have
gone ahead is instructive. In part, he reaches this conclusion
because he regards the case as involving speech and adopts

the orthodox First Amendment position that viewpoint-based restrictions on free speech are always impermissible. 'No one can validly prevent the public advocacy (in appropriate time, place and manner)', he writes, 'of any political opinions, no matter how odious' (p. 86). The main reason behind Feinberg's defence of the Nazis' right to march, however, is that, because the march was announced in advance, it was easy to avoid (p. 87). Had the Nazis marched more frequently or at irregular times, or mingled with shoppers in the mall, he says, our conclusions should be different.

But this reasoning raises the question of why reasonable avoidability should be granted such a central place among the criteria that favour the liberty to engage in profoundly offensive conduct. Why not prioritise the fact that the march was motivated by malice and spite, a criterion that, Feinberg says, detracts from one's liberty to be offensive? Moreover, even if the march was easy to avoid, this does not mean that it was *reasonably* avoidable. Why should the Jews of Skokie have remained hidden away in their homes during the march? The town was theirs to inhabit, not the visiting Nazis' to parade through.

Feinberg's treatment of the Skokie case also highlights the problems that arise with any analysis of offence that does not include some reference to reasonableness. Feinberg considers the reverse argument, that racist whites might have been profoundly offended by civil rights marchers in Harlem, and defends the latter's right to march on the grounds that there was no threat of violence, no gratuitous affront to what is held sacred, and no association with historical killings – as with the Nazis or the Ku Klux Klan (KKK) (p. 93). As we suggested above, it would be far easier to say that the civil rights demonstration should have been allowed because it sought to uphold the values of freedom and equality, and therefore was reasonable, while KKK and Nazi marches are unreasonable because they deny the free and equal status of certain citizens. On this view, reasonableness and unreasonableness amount to the endorsement or the denial of other citizens' free and equal status. This view is counterbalanced by the First Amendment view that it is illegitimate for the neutral liberal state to adopt a normative position by circumscribing what citizens wish to express (and how they express it).

We can also look at the Skokie case through the lens of the three arguments for free speech. First, on the consequentialist argument, there seems to be no reason to think that the march would have enabled anyone to arrive more easily at the truth. The serious risk that its offensiveness could have escalated into hate speech (if it was not already that) meant that it would have been very difficult for members of the Jewish community and other inhabitants of Skokie to see it as a stimulus for reasoned deliberation aimed at discovering the truth. On the autonomy-based view, we are left balancing the autonomy of the Nazis to march with the autonomy of Skokie's Jews, who would have been impeded in their daily life activities had the march gone ahead.

Finally, on the democratic argument, it is hard to argue that Nazi marches contribute much to public discussion. They may earn their organisers publicity, but the fear and intimidation that they bring are hardly conducive to public debate or to granting a democratic voice to Jewish people (such as Skokie's Jewish residents). Moreover, the various ordinances issued by the Village of Skokie against the proposed march were the result of deliberation among its citizens; the majority of them eventually decided that prohibiting the march was the right thing to do. The decision to regulate free speech was therefore clearly a democratic one, which Skokie's inhabitants had an interest in protecting.

To conclude our analysis of Feinberg's theory of offence, let us briefly return to the *Jyllands-Posten* cartoons controversy examined earlier. The cartoons are of course an instance of offence to moral or religious sensibilities and easily pass the threshold of profound offence. For Feinberg, a judgement call on the cartoons would be determined by a number of factors, including the intensity of the offence caused and the newspaper's motives. Were its journalists genuinely interested in sparking debate on free speech and censorship, or were they motivated by spite and malice? Or was it a combination of both? From a Feinbergian point of view, a significant problem with the call for censorship of the cartoons is that many of the Muslims who protested had not seen them; so this would seem to be a case of bare knowledge offence, which Feinberg rules out (cf. Jones 2011, p. 86) – an issue similar to that around *Jerry Springer: The Opera* and *The Satanic Verses.*

However, the notion of bare knowledge offence needs to be considered with care. It would indeed be unreasonable to be offended by the mere knowledge of what others are doing behind closed doors. Self-regarding or self-oriented behaviour of this kind is exactly what Mill's harm principle is designed to protect. But, in all the examples we have considered, what the offended parties really object to is the public treatment of their deep commitments – religious, moral or of any other nature – as in the case of flag burning. Newspapers, books, theatre performances, TV programmes, websites and the like express attitudes not through self-regarding behaviour but through what they convey to a relatively wide audience, and such attitudes incorporate messages of respect or disrespect. Even those who have not seen or read the offending message will come to know about disrespectful attitudes, and it is to that treatment of their convictions that they object. Thus, in the case of the Danish cartoons, though the original source of Muslim objections was the offensive way in which Islam had been portrayed in *Jyllands-Posten*, as the issue was more widely publicised the real object of anger came to be the public disrespect shown towards Muslims' beliefs; and it was not necessary to see the cartoons in order to experience this anger (Jones 2011, pp. 86–9). The same applies to the other cases of offence that we have considered in this chapter.

It makes some sense to dismiss private bare knowledge offence – where someone is offended by the mere thought that a norm she holds dear is disregarded by others – but controversial cases of this type have a more public, expressive nature. We previously suggested employing a reasonableness test to defend the asymmetry between liberal-minded citizens and citizens with extremist views; such a test could be applied to public bare knowledge offences as well. But, while the test has some bite, it will not always offer decisive guidance, and on competing religious worldviews, for example, will do so only rarely. Since there are on occasion good reasons behind speech or conduct that foreseeably offends, cases of offence – profound religious offence in particular – generate some of the most intractable controversies that surround free speech.

5
Pornography

Introduction

While issues of hateful and offensive speech dominate contemporary debates on free speech, earlier debates paid heed to yet another important and divisive area: pornography. In the past two decades the dramatic rise of pornographic videos and images on the Internet, and hence the sheer volume of material easily available to the consumer, have reignited controversy on this subject. One of the main implications of the development of online pornography is that pornography is no longer a discreet activity that happens in the shadows but one that has been mainstreamed and normalised. Empirical data show, for example, that over 70 per cent of college students in Sweden, Canada, Germany and the United States have viewed online pornography. The percentages for adolescent boys in Sweden and Taiwan are respectively 96 and 74 per cent. Furthermore, 80 per cent of men and 50 per cent of women in Australia have accessed pornographic material on the Internet. In 2017 Pornhub, the most accessed online pornography website, recorded more than 3,732 petabytes (i.e. more than 3 billion gigabytes) of downloads (Grubbs et al. 2019). This renders the analysis of the relationship between pornography and free speech particularly urgent. In the present chapter we survey this relationship and show how the debate around it raises issues about harm similar to those we found in the hate speech debate. Caroline West has recently defined pornography as 'sexually explicit material (verbal or pictorial) *that is primarily designed to produce sexual arousal in viewers*' and '*that is bad* in a certain way' (West 2018). This useful definition captures three important features of pornography. First, it highlights the main purpose of pornographic material, namely causing sexual arousal. But, second, West's use of the word 'primarily' suggests that pornography can have other purposes too or, more broadly, does other things too. As we shall see, some feminist writers hold that pornography is not merely a mode of expression but also a type of action – specifically, the act of subordinating women – and, relatedly, that an effect (if not the purpose) of pornography is to encourage violence, harassment and discrimination against women, issues clearly important in the debate about its regulation. As well as causing sexual arousal, at least some pornography may also convey an artistic or political message that is worth hearing. If this statement is correct, conveying such messages is another purpose. Third, West's definition is a moralised one, as it considers pornography wrong, while leaving open why that is the case. This attitude accords with our everyday intuition that pornography is morally problematic, but in a way that invites specification rather than being obvious. Articulating what pornography's moral wrongness might involve is the main goal of this chapter.

In what follows we limit the discussion to heterosexual pornography involving women. We do not consider other varieties, such as gay pornography or child pornography (the latter is simply child abuse). After briefly considering conservative and communitarian arguments about pornography, we examine this topic from the perspective of the liberal argument from truth, and then investigate at some length the various harms associated with pornography. We conclude by considering the relationship between pornography and the autonomy and democracy arguments for free speech: as in hate speech, while pornography might sometimes serve the corresponding values (i.e. autonomy and democracy), it will more commonly undermine them.

Conservative and communitarian arguments

Conservative arguments for the regulation of pornography, though less popular nowadays, still play some role, especially among those who embrace traditional conceptions of morality rooted in religious worldviews. The conservative position is often identified with legal moralism – the idea that the state's role is to maintain a traditional moral ethos and to prevent it from becoming degraded or corrupted. As the conservative judge Lord Devlin held in his famous book *The Enforcement of Morals*, 'what makes a society of any sort is community of ideas, not only political ideas but also ideas about the way its members should behave and govern their lives' (Devlin 1968, p. 9). On this view, pornography is dangerous because it betrays those ideas and damages '[t]he moral fabric of society' (Warburton 2009, p. 70) regardless of whether it causes any harm to others. And if pornography transgresses society's shared moral code, it can legitimately be penalised, even if not everyone actually shares that code. This conception clearly justifies a much higher level of state intervention in the lives of individual citizens than Mill's harm principle would warrant.

Related to this conservative position are arguments grounded in communitarianism, the view that human beings are shaped by the communities in which they live (e.g. family, nation) and have special duties and obligations towards them (Bell 2020). For example, Michael Sandel (1984, p. 17) has argued that '[c]ommunitarians would be more likely than liberals to allow a town to ban pornographic bookstores, on the grounds that pornography offends its way of life and the values that sustain it'. If we have an obligation to sustain the community that we inhabit, and if we think that the widespread presence of pornographic materials (nowadays largely online, not in bookstores) undermines values that hold communities together, then on this view pornography may be banned or regulated.

Aspects of the conservative and communitarian views are reflected in the way in which pornography is legally defined as obscenity in some jurisdictions, for instance in the Obscene Publications Act in the United Kingdom (see Parliament of the United Kingdom 1959). The Act proscribes material that has a 'tendency to deprave or corrupt' its viewers: this kind of language sounds quaintly old-fashioned today.

Likewise, in the case of *Miller v California* (1973), which concerned a pornographic bookseller, the US Supreme Court provided a set of criteria for assessing when speech counts as obscenity and could therefore be permissibly regulated:

> The basic guidelines for the trier of fact must be: (a) whether 'the average person, applying contemporary community standards' would find that the work ... appeals to the prurient interest ... (b) whether the work depicts or describes, in a patently offensive way, sexual conduct specifically defined by the applicable state law, and (c) whether the work, taken as a whole, lacks serious literary, artistic, political, or scientific value. If a state obscenity law is thus limited, First Amendment values are adequately protected by ultimate independent appellate review of constitutional claims when necessary. (*Miller v California*, 1973)

One central problem for the conservative and communitarian arguments against pornography is that in contemporary, diverse societies characterised by value disagreements it is unclear by whose standards legal authorities can legitimately judge whether pornographic material is obscene or offensive. Taking religious or specifically Christian views as an anchor (as is evident in Devlin's work) would not be supported by citizens who do not share them. As a result, to regulate pornography on the grounds that it offends a traditional conservative or Christian viewpoint, or a community's values, would be to limit some people's liberty on grounds that they could not reasonably accept; and this is an illegitimate restriction from a liberal perspective (Rawls 2005).

Pornography and truth

Liberal and feminist arguments against pornography are rooted in the harm it inflicts on others, specifically women. But, before examining those arguments, we pause to consider whether pornography might enjoy some social value as a means of conveying possible truths about human nature and society. In Chapter 1 we discussed a version of the truth argument where free speech should be protected on the grounds that it stimulates our deliberative capacities and our ability to reason our way to better founded views. Put that way, the truth-based argument for pornography sounds unpromising. As Schauer (1982, p. 181) points out, '[a]t its most extreme, hard core pornography is a sex aid, no more and no less'. On this view, there is little sense in which pornography communicates ideas that rational persons might discuss. Such a view is reflected in the landmark US case *Roth v United States* (1957), where the Supreme Court held that obscene pornographic material was 'utterly without redeeming social importance' and therefore beyond the scope of the First Amendment; by contrast, unorthodox or controversial views, or 'even ideas hateful to the prevailing climate of opinion', enjoy First Amendment protection. Although the Court did not put things this way, this amounts to saying that controversial ideas, but not obscene pornographic material, may help us to arrive at the truth. The *Roth* decision prepared the ground for the later verdict in *Miller v California* (1973), to which we return now.

If we consider prong (c) of the *Miller* test ('whether the work, taken as a whole, lacks serious literary, artistic, political, or scientific value'), we see a possible truth-based defence of pornographic speech. While most pornography would lack literary, artistic or political value, some might possess a little value, and therefore be defensible on the grounds that it contributes to society's public conversation, for example by implicitly or explicitly advancing the view that certain forms of sexual expression are worth engaging in and celebrating. Here we can also employ the distinction mentioned earlier (p. 4) between high-value and low-value speech. It is easy to see how most pornography falls into the latter category; but some of it may count as high-value speech. That part of it would be worthy of protection because, like any other high-value expression, for example aesthetic or political, it has some artistic or even literary elements, and therefore stimulates our thought (but compare Easton 1995, p. 36).

One example of potentially high-value pornography is

Pier Paolo Pasolini's movie *Salò, or the 120 Days of Sodom*, released in 1975 but still banned in many countries to this day, at least in the uncut version, on account of its graphic portrayal of sexual acts, violence and sadism involving adults and teenagers. Yet, as pointed out by the British philosopher Bernard Williams, who chaired the influential Home Office Committee on Obscenity and Film Censorship, although the movie 'has the ritual form of a pornographic work' and some Committee members 'were ... suspicious of its intentions', it could also be considered 'an extraordinary metaphor of political power' (Williams 2015, p. 143), showing that seemingly pornographic material can be used to convey a profound political message.

Further, the very boundary between art and pornography can be contested on cultural grounds as well. In 2013, for example, the British Museum hosted an exhibition of Japanese shunga (literally 'spring picture') prints, a type of erotic art. The exhibition included paintings that many considered pornographic by virtue of their ability to cause sexual arousal; but the same paintings also seemed to contain artistic elements. As the exhibition curator stated at the time, '[i]n the west, we have created a state of affairs where there has to be a firewall between art and pornography ... [b]ut Shunga is both sexually explicit and demonstrably art'.[1] The distinctive western approach to the relationship between art and pornography, he said, is due to the fact that, in Europe, 'since at least the Renaissance ... prevailing religious and social bans have made it well-nigh impossible for leading artists to produce works that are explicitly erotic'.[2] This has a more general implication. In line with the argument for free speech (mentioned in Chapter 1) that is grounded in scepticism about governments' appropriate use of coercive power, one argument against the regulation of pornography is that governments will not reliably distinguish between the kinds of harmful pornography that should definitely be banned and those that almost certainly should not be – like the provocative paintings in the shunga exhibition.

Nonetheless, even if some pornography includes high-value speech, one might still argue that its regulation is permissible within the bounds of the truth-based argument for free speech (see Easton 1994, pp. 54–6). Pornography may do little to help us exchange error for truth if it contains much that is erroneous, distorted, one-sided, and even pernicious about intimate relations between men and women and about the gendered division of social roles. There is a legitimate debate on the merits of sexual promiscuity versus the more conservative view that sexual intercourse should take place only within monogamous marriages. But even if some pornography implicitly advocates the former, that message will be obscured if it also portrays all women – and, for that matter, men – as always ready for sex. This is a harmful stereotype, or even an instance of group defamation, akin to the harms that hate speech inflicts on racial and other minorities (Brown 2015, pp. 113–14). In any assessment of the worth of regulating pornography, these kinds of harms need to be weighed against the benefits of truth discovery – just as in the case of hate speech. Indeed, the sheer pervasiveness of pornography in society plausibly inflicts all sorts of harms, which may well outweigh whatever benefits it brings to the process of arriving at truths about human sexuality, especially when there are many non-pornographic ways in which such truths can be expressed. We now turn to assessing the harms of pornography.

Pornography and harm

We saw how legal and political theorists have developed very fine-grained and nuanced accounts of the various harms that hate speech inflicts. In the context of the debate around pornography there are parallel, indeed partly overlapping views as to its harmfulness. Just as in our discussion of hate speech, then, we need to examine the sorts of harms pornography may inflict on women and through what sorts of processes. In this section we survey the four principal contenders: pornography can cause sexual violence against women; it can coerce, exploit and otherwise harm the women involved in its production; it can demean or subordinate women in society more generally; and it can silence women's voices.

One widely recognised reason for limiting hate speech is

its connection with incitement to violence. Could a similar reason justify the regulation of pornography? Even though violent pornographic material may not be produced with the intention of inciting violence, the moral test is whether it is likely to do so. Here it is useful to distinguish between short- and long-term effects. Among the former, the typical example is that of men already predisposed to violence who watch violent pornography and shortly afterwards commit rape or sexual assault. But such cases represent a small proportion of those in which women are victims of male violence, and causation is difficult to prove: it could be that a man already intending to commit violence against a woman chose to watch violent pornography first. The more common long-term harm accusation is that prolonged exposure to hardcore pornography, even of a non-violent kind, is *a* significant factor in explaining male violence against women. Some feminists – including Catharine MacKinnon, the standard-bearer of the anti-pornography movement – defend that connection. Commenting on the violence that, she believes, is inherent in all pornography, MacKinnon writes:

> Sooner or later, in one way or another, the consumers want to live out the pornography further in three dimensions. Sooner or later, in one way or another, they do. It makes them want to; when they believe they can, when they feel they can get away with it, they do. (MacKinnon 1993, p. 19)

But this statement, interpreted literally, cannot be right (cf. Dworkin 1993, p. 38). Most male consumers of pornography do not commit sexual violence, and perpetrators of sexual violence may well not view pornography.[3] For the claim that pornography causes violence against women to be plausible, therefore, the relevant notion of causation must be a probabilistic one: the existence of pornography makes it *more likely* that sexual crimes against women will be committed, but it does not determine them any more than the fact that a person is a heavy smoker determines that she will get cancer (Eaton 2007, pp. 696–7; Watson 2010, p. 543).

Interpreted this way, is the long-term harm argument plausible? Some early studies, such as the Williams Committee Report that we mentioned earlier, suggested that it was not.

By contrast, the 1986 US Attorney General's Commission on Pornography found that the evidence it surveyed 'strongly supports' a causal relationship between substantial exposure to sexually violent material and real acts of sexual violence, although the Commission was criticised on the grounds that it was set up by the Reagan administration precisely in order to arrive at a conservative conclusion (Meese Report, cited in MacKinnon 2017, p. 99; see also Dworkin 1993, p. 36). More recent studies have relied upon a variety of social scientific methods that include victim testimony, laboratory studies of the effect of pornography on male respondents' attitudes, and studies of male sex offenders (Watson 2010, p. 543). While the conclusions are by no means beyond dispute, some contemporary meta-analyses (comparative analyses of analyses of the relationship between pornography and sexual violence) have found a positive correlation (Hald et al. 2010; Wright et al. 2016). If correct, this evidence would support the legal regulation of violent pornography. Interestingly, however, one study found a lack of evidence for the thesis that greater availability of pornography via the Internet over the past two decades has resulted in a higher correlation with sexual violence (Wright et al. 2016, p. 194).

The case of violence raises the issue of a second kind of harm: harm to the women who participate in the production of pornography. While the apparent violence displayed in some hardcore pornography may be simulated, even simulation will carry certain risks, and in any case much violent pornography is a true depiction of painful and physically dangerous acts committed on its female participants. Some pornography contains not so much physical harm, but scenes of humiliation, such as being treated as a slave. Furthermore, women whose partners upload to pornographic websites sexually explicit images of them without their consent are humiliated too, as well as having their privacy invaded. These are clear harms. This is why what is called 'revenge porn' is a specific criminal offence, for example in the United Kingdom, Japan and elsewhere.[4] A final category of harm to the women involved in the production of pornography is economic. It is often said that pornography is one of the few industries where women earn more than men, but this is not invariably true. As in sports and other forms of entertainment, in pornography, too, there is a great range of salaries and top stars may earn a great deal, but many earn very little. In addition, the careers of most female actors or models are relatively short, and the stigma of having worked in the pornographic industry can make it hard to secure employment afterwards. Finally, a significant number of young women are abducted or trafficked into the pornographic industry, where they are coerced to participate in sexual acts with men. They are threatened or blackmailed if they try to leave.

The latter point raises important moral issues of consent. Normally we believe that, if a person genuinely consents to an act in full knowledge of what it involves, then she cannot be harmed by it. Consent is a liberal value, and it is important for feminists too; in matters of sex, it marks the moral boundary between voluntary sexual intercourse and rape. Applying the consent principle to the examples we adduced here would appear to permit situations in which women are consensually subjected to pain or humiliation or economically exploited; and only cases of threat, blackmail, trafficking and revenge porn would seem to be ruled out. After all, speech (in its widest sense) is valuable only when freely engaged in; coerced speech is not free speech.

But even if at least some women consent to participating in pornography, should they be paternalistically prevented from doing so for their own good? The answer to this question is complicated. Many women who become involved in the pornographic industry, perhaps gradually, may do so without full knowledge of what they are becoming engulfed in. Even if this is not deliberate manipulation by male pornographers, it still erodes the moral force of the consent principle. Further, participating in a practice which substantially sets back one's interests reduces the value of consent if the alternative to doing so is an option which is worse still. As in the case of prostitution, some women who turn to pornography to make a living probably enjoy few social and economic opportunities elsewhere. They may be homeless or living in poverty. This draws attention to broader issues of social justice that are often bound up with the question of free speech (see Dworkin 1993; Wendell 1983).

The last two categories of harm that pornography is

enmeshed with – subordination and silencing – can best be understood by drawing on the work of the academic lawyer Catharine MacKinnon. MacKinnon, together with the anti-pornography writer and activist Andrea Dworkin, drafted the much discussed Antipornography Civil Rights Ordinance in the 1980s (Dworkin and MacKinnon 1983). The Ordinance conceptualised pornography as a civil wrong, empowering women to sue for damages in civil courts; it did not make it a criminal act, since criminalising pornography, in MacKinnon's view, would merely drive it underground. The Ordinance defined pornography as a 'systematic practice of exploitation and subordination based on sex that differentially harms and disadvantages women'.[5] Initially enacted in Indianapolis and other US cities, the Ordinance was eventually struck down by US courts as unconstitutional, on the grounds that it did not meet any of the three criteria of *Miller v California* (1973) and that portraying women as submissive or as enjoying humiliation was viewpoint-specific and hence protected by the First Amendment. Here is how MacKinnon summarises her view of pornography:

> With the rape and prostitution in which it participates, pornography institutionalizes the sexuality of male supremacy, which fuses the erotization of dominance and submission with the social construction of male and female. Gender is sexual. Pornography constitutes the meaning of that sexuality. Men treat women as who they see women as being. Pornography constructs who that is. Men's power over women means that the way men see women defines who women can be. Pornography is that way. (MacKinnon 1984, p. 326)

To understand this passage, we need to make a distinction between sex difference as a biological category and sex difference as a gendered category. That women and men differ physically tells us little (if anything) about the norms and expectations that define their gendered roles. This becomes evident if we compare their respective roles in liberal, egalitarian societies and in more religiously conservative ones. MacKinnon objects to the subordinate role that women occupy even in relatively liberal societies; she also sees pornography as having a key role in constructing this status, both through women's own beliefs about their appropriate social roles and through men's expectations of those roles; the confluence of these two factors keeps in place a pervasive system of gendered subordination, just what feminists seek to combat. It is worth noting that one could reject the feminist view of gendered roles and still object to pornography; indeed this is precisely the conservative line, according to which pornography damages traditional values rather than harming women. By contrast, MacKinnon's view is that 'the harm of pornography, broadly speaking, is the harm of the civil inequality of the sexes made invisible as harm' (MacKinnon 1987, p. 178). It is made invisible insofar as gendered roles appear to us as natural features of the social landscape.

Subordination undermines equality, a central value for feminists and liberals; but there are several ways in which the subordination of women in pornography can be understood. One way, inspired by the wording of the Ordinance, involves considering subordination as a source of humiliation, which demeans or denigrates its victims. Although this approach fails to respect the US principle of viewpoint neutrality, in *R v Butler* (1992) the Canadian Supreme Court held that pornographic material of a degrading or dehumanising nature could be legitimately censored. MacKinnon's claim that 'men treat women as who they see women as being' also appeals to a second, causal sense of subordination. On her argument, the widespread consumption of pornography is partly responsible for a multitude of civil harms to which women are subject – for example harassment, discrimination, inequality of opportunity, lack of political voice, and sexist and misogynistic attitudes more generally. Pornography also enables the male domination of women in multiple spheres of contemporary society: social, economic, political, familial – and the list goes on. This causal interpretation of subordination looks like the harm-based argument we encountered earlier, where pornography is said to provoke some men to commit sexual violence against women, an argument MacKinnon also makes. Undoubtedly there is overlap between the two, but the violence argument is focused on a narrow class of harms committed by a relatively small number of men, whereas the scope of the subordination argument is far broader: this argument claims that pornography, through shaping the very categories of gender, is responsible for institutionalising male dominance over women and the latter's sense of inferiority. Put simply, pornography keeps in place the basic social hierarchy of sexism.

A partly related argument, informed by virtue ethics and, more specifically, by the philosophy of Alasdair MacIntyre, is based on the idea that the good life for human beings involves realising certain moral virtues, for example courage, generosity, truthfulness or justice. MacIntyre's defence of virtue ethics is complex and we can only sketch its bare outline here. According to him, virtues are embedded in social practices such as performing in an orchestra, playing chess, playing football, or building houses. In general, a practice is 'any coherent and complex form of socially established cooperative human activity through which goods internal to that form of activity are realized in the course of trying to achieve those standards of excellence which are appropriate to, and partially definitive of, that form of activity' (MacIntyre 1984, p. 187). Thus chess, music, sports and building all have standards of excellence associated with them; by seeking to meet those standards, we achieve the good of the practice. A virtue, for MacIntyre, is 'an acquired human quality the possession and exercise of which tends to enable us to achieve those goods which are internal to practices and the lack of which effectively prevents us from achieving any such goods' (p. 191). Players' sense of fairness is a virtue of sports and games, for example: participants cannot achieve the good of those practices without it. According to Strikwerda (2017), sex could also be understood as a practice in MacIntyre's sense, one to which 'reflexive mutual recognition of desire by desire' (Ruddick 1975, p. 89) is central, since sexual partners 'actively desire and respond to each other's active desires' (pp. 89–90). Pornographic sexual relationships lack this reciprocity, since they involve the subordination of women to men. They are therefore harmful from the perspective of virtue ethics; 'they erode the virtue of respect for persons' (Strikwerda 2017, p. 140).

Having said all that, the view that pornography keeps in place the basic social hierarchy of sexism seems overstated. How about men who eschew pornography? What is the process by which they assimilate gendered norms? How about gendered societies, such as in the Middle East, where there is relatively little pornography? Indeed, most societies throughout human history have been deeply gendered in the absence of mass pornography. However, it is important to understand that, unlike the violence argument, the subordination argument need not posit any concrete relationship between the consumption of pornography and particular acts committed by particular men. Rather it claims that, as a social practice, pornography shapes our interpretation of gender roles so as to maintain a system of gender inequality and female subordination. Nor need MacKinnon claim that pornography is the *only* practice responsible for these systemic features. She claims instead that pornography is an especially pernicious cause of gender inequality in the United States and similar societies. As Cynthia Stark explains in her analysis of MacKinnon's argument, 'pornography combines a particularly damaging and invidious message with a particularly potent method of conveyance', namely the fact that it is sexually arousing, and hence it is 'especially critical to the construction of gender and sexuality in ways that help constitute male dominance' (Stark 1997, p. 294). Stark herself, however, is somewhat sceptical of MacKinnon's claim that pornography is especially salient in constructing gender inequality. According to her, Christianity contains an equally damaging view of women, according to which their role is to serve men and bear 'their' children (p. 299).

There are two responses that an advocate of the subordination argument could offer to Stark's analogy. First, a feminist who agreed with the analogy could argue that all it shows is that the battle for gender equality has to be fought on multiple fronts: regulating and seeking to limit the consumption of pornography is one; encouraging more liberal-minded interpretations of Christianity is another; vigorously pursuing laws against discrimination and harassment in employment is yet another – and so on. But, second, a liberal who agreed with the analogy might argue that all it shows is that, just as much Christian doctrine is valuable even if some of it is outdated in today's world, so *some* pornography is an instance of high-value speech even if most of it conveys a message that many abhor. By contrast,

MacKinnon's view is that pornography is utterly without redeeming social value.

In fact there is yet another version of the subordination argument that is subtly distinct from the causal version we have just considered. Although it appeals to the same basic intuition that pornography is an attack on sex and gender equality, the conceptual argument, as Stark (1997) calls it, develops MacKinnon's claim that 'pornography is what it does, not what it says'. According to the conceptual argument, pornography *is* the act of ranking women as subordinate. This point is separate from, though of course closely related to, the claim that pornography contributes to *causing* women's subordination in society. It has been put across, with considerable theoretical sophistication, by the Australian philosopher Rae Langton (1993), in what she takes to be an elaboration on MacKinnon's view. Drawing on the philosophy of language, Langton distinguishes between the perlocutionary dimension of an act of freedom of speech – or speech act, as philosophers call it – and its illocutionary force. The perlocutionary aspect of a speech act refers to the fact that an act produces an effect on its audience; for example, if someone swears at you, you feel offended or, if someone shows a pornographic film, the audience gets sexually aroused. The illocutionary force of a speech act refers to the fact that expressing something can sometimes constitute a special kind of action in itself. If a marriage registrar says to a couple, at their wedding, 'I now pronounce you husband and wife', she is not seeking to persuade the audience that the couple are now married; rather that speech act *itself* constitutes the act of marrying two people. Likewise, Langton points out, taking an example from MacKinnon, a racist sign that says 'whites only' is not simply a perlocutionary speech act that has the effect of barring black individuals from certain areas. It is also an illocutionary act that *ranks* blacks as second-class citizens, thereby subordinating them and legitimating further causal effects, such as discrimination.

Pornography, on Langton's view, is, similarly, an illocutionary act of subordination. Pornography *is* the act of ranking women as inferior to men by portraying them in a demeaning way, as sex objects for men's pleasure, and it therefore legitimates further acts that harm women such as sexual violence, just as the racist sign legitimates discrimination and violence. In fact Langton goes further. The illocutionary force of certain speech acts can extend to depriving individuals of certain rights and powers. Thus an individual, once married, is not (legally) free to marry a second partner; black citizens in apartheid South Africa were denied the legal right to vote by that country's white legislators, and so on.

Further, Langton argues that pornography is the speech act that, as a result of attacking the normative status of women, also deprives them of speech. It does not do it causally, by threatening or coercing women, though pornography may well achieve that too. Rather Langton's view – also expressed in her work with Jennifer Hornsby – is that pornography, as an illocutionary act, silences women by undermining the illocutionary force of their speech acts, in particular acts of refusal or discussion about sex. Women are thus silenced through a process of 'illocutionary disablement': their speech systematically 'misfires' (Hornsby and Langton 1998, p. 21), since their illocutionary acts fail to secure uptake.

In a slightly different version of the argument, Ishani Maitra (2009) characterises the silencing effect of pornography as an instance of *communicative* (as opposed to *illocutionary*) disablement. Communicative disablement, Maitra argues, occurs when a speaker's communicative intentions are unfulfilled; for example, a woman's informed intention not to have sex with a man fails to be recognised by him (pp. 326–7). Yet another version of the silencing argument is defended by Mary Kate McGowan (2009). According to her, pornography can silence women even when there is no communicative failure. It can do so when it leads male consumers to believe that women are sexual objects that do not have the necessary *authority* to refuse sexual advances. In this scenario there is no communicative interference per se – and for this reason, McGowan argues, there is no actual infringement of women's free speech rights; yet pornography still silences, and is therefore harmful to women.

Speech acts, just like refusal and protest, make sense only if they are understood by those to whom they are directed. If, as MacKinnon (1992, p. 483) says, pornography 'strips and devastates women of credibility', then their protests against sexual violence will go unheard. If men have sex with women against their will in pornographic films, then the notions of women's consent and women's refusal become emptied of meaning. According to MacKinnon (1992, p. 484), '[w]e are stripped of authority and reduced and devalidated and silenced' by pornography.

In summary, pornography's silencing of women can operate in different ways (West 2018). First, a hostile political environment can make women reluctant to speak out, especially on those issues where male power is most stark – such as harassment, voyeurism, discrimination and sexual crime. Second, pornography reduces women's credibility and authority when they engage in public speech, and as a result their views may be more easily dismissed. Thus a male politician's ideas of what counts as harassment may often be taken more seriously than those of his female colleagues. Third, pornography can cause women's speech not to be properly comprehended; it can even frustrate women's very capacity to express their thoughts. For instance, when the crucial distinction between consent and refusal has been obscured through the influence of pornography, a woman who speaks out against harassment might be seen as rejecting all male sexual attention.

For MacKinnon, silencing means that pornography is really action, not speech, and hence falls outside the protection offered by the First Amendment. By analogy, the 'whites only' sign is an act of discrimination or segregation, and thus not protected speech either. Further, just as the racist sign is incompatible with the Fourteenth Amendment to the US Constitution, which guarantees civil equality, so too is pornography. For MacKinnon, pornography violates the Fourteenth Amendment because it subordinates women.

The conceptual argument and its dimension of silencing, like other versions of the subordination argument, can be criticised on a number of grounds. One criticism is that it seems implausible that pornography can really silence all women in the requisite normative sense. According to these critics, silencing, as a form of illocutionary disablement, is possible only if the silencer enjoys a special form of authority. It is true that male pornographers possess some authority over the women who work in pornography, but to extrapolate from that so as to claim that *all* women are silenced in the sense of being unheard is a substantial and perhaps unwarranted step (McKinnon 2006, pp. 148–50). Another criticism takes a more or less opposite stand. It points to other domains beside pornography where one group's speech acts subordinate another. For Stark (as we saw), religion is one such domain. Thus, if the conceptual argument is taken as grounds for outlawing pornography or for regulating only certain modes of speech but not others, it may be overbroad.

Pornography and autonomy

When we discussed the autonomy argument for free speech, we paid attention to the autonomy of the receivers of speech and to that of third parties – and not just to the autonomy of speakers. A similar range of perspectives applies in the case of pornography. On the one hand, the right to produce and consume pornography could be defended in terms of autonomy; on the other, we cast doubt on whether some women's decision to work in the pornography industry is genuinely autonomous. We must also consider the effect of pornography on women's autonomy in wider society.

These perspectives can be illustrated by returning to Ronald Dworkin's autonomy-based argument for the right to moral independence. Dworkin (1981) argues that this right rules out strict limitations on the availability of pornography. Central to Dworkin's (1977) general argument is the idea that in a liberal state public policy should not be shaped by citizens' *external* preferences, that is, by preferences about how other people should live their lives, since these kinds of preferences fail to treat citizens with equal concern and respect. Turning now to pornography, according to Dworkin, individuals who want to outlaw it on the grounds that other citizens' consumption of it is 'ignoble or wrong', or reflects their 'bad character' (Dworkin 1981, p. 196), appeal to external preferences. Such judgements are reminiscent of conservative and legal moralist views and are ruled out by the right to moral independence. (It is important to note that

Dworkin does favour some regulation of pornography on other grounds.)

However, as Rae Langton (1990) has powerfully argued, the preference to consume and enjoy pornography *is itself* an external preference of the type that Dworkin rules out. If the subordination arguments we considered are correct, the preference for pornography is grounded in the view that women are inferior to men; and this, Langton maintains, is contrary to Dworkin's core principle of equal concern and respect. Hence '[w]omen as a group have rights against the consumers of pornography, and thereby have rights that are trumps against the policy of permitting pornography' (p. 346). On the assumption that society-wide subordination damages women's capacity to direct their own lives, Langton's reply neatly shows how autonomy cuts both ways in the pornography debate, just as it does in the discussion of hate speech.

Scanlon's (1972) original autonomy argument – according to which responsibility lies with the autonomous person who receives others' speech, and not with those others who deliver it – also has important implications for the analysis of pornography. Even when receiving speech results in a person's committing a harm, it is that (autonomous) person who decides how she acts on the basis of what she hears, sees or reads. This implies that, *even if* one could prove that consuming pornography leads some men to harm women, it would still be impermissible to censor it on those grounds, because individuals are responsible for what they believe and for how they act as a result. In a later article, Scanlon developed a more nuanced account of our interests in free speech, including the interests of third parties ('bystanders'), which can be set back by others' speech. In this revised argument he maintains that, while 'partisans of pornography' are entitled to 'a fair opportunity to influence the sexual mores of the[ir] society' (Scanlon 1979, p. 545) by using pornographic materials as a way of promoting their view of sex, there are still grounds for regulation, if their aim is 'only to appeal to a prurient interest in sex' (p. 546). Further, he wondered whether his original autonomy argument was not 'overly cognitive and rationalistic', since pornography may influence our tastes and preferences in ways 'outside of one's rational control' (p. 547), not unlike subliminal advertising. If and when it does, perhaps pornography has an undue influence on at least some of its male consumers, undermining their autonomy.

We distinguished between autonomy as a moral attribute to be respected, as in Dworkin's and Scanlon's earlier argument, and autonomy as a substantive capacity to be promoted, as in Scanlon's later argument. Other contemporary liberal theorists (e.g. Raz 1986) endorse the latter view as well; but its supporters are not limited to contemporary theorists. We drew attention to the way in which Mill's argument from truth hinges on the use of our deliberative capacities for thought and reflection, so that we do not receive 'truths' through indoctrination. In this way, the truth and autonomy arguments partially overlap. As we noted in Chapter 1, Mill's character ideal of individuality, in which we are enjoined to develop our 'strong natures', think for ourselves, be independent-minded, and conduct 'experiments in living', is very similar to our modern conception of substantive autonomy.

In his reconstruction of what Mill's attitude towards pornography would be, David Dyzenhaus (1992) argues cogently that we need to consider *On Liberty* in conjunction with Mill's 1869 feminist work *The Subjection of Women* (Mill 2006). There Mill argues that the subordination of women to men that was central to Victorian society is morally unjust and should give way to greater gender equality. Dyzenhaus maintains that, by 'eroticizing inequality', pornography would count as a harm in Mill's judgement because it 'makes an inequality which is ultimately rooted in superior physical power and thus in physical coercion appear sexually desirable' and, moreover, it helps cement inequality as 'the regime which prevents women from articulating and living out conceptions of the good life which rival those that patriarchy rules appropriate' (Dyzenhaus 1992, p. 5). Put another way, pornography contributes to sustaining the systematic subordination that stifles women's individuality, and therefore their flourishing (cf. Easton 1994). This puts Mill in touch with the contemporary feminist arguments around subordination.

In summary, while the autonomy argument provides some

reasons to favour a more libertarian position on pornography, given that women's right to an autonomous life is just as important as men's, the balance shifts towards supporting a more interventionist position.

Pornography and democracy

A similar balance, with competing normative considerations on both sides, is at work if we consider pornography in the context of the democratic argument for free speech. At first glance, pornography does not appear to make any significant contribution to democratic debate of the kind we outlined in Chapter 1. Yet one could argue that pornography can convey ideas – for example about sexuality – that are relevant to political debate and decision-making. This, after all, is Scanlon's point: pornographers should have the right to influence citizens' views on sexuality in their society, a topic with important potential implications for debates on key issues such as abortion, divorce, gay marriage, contraception, age of sexual consent, transgender rights, and so on. If a person wants to use pornography to persuade others to embrace his or her views on such issues, the democracy argument seems to imply that this use of pornography should count as protected speech.

But, as we pointed out, whether pornography is protected speech depends somewhat on the motivation of pornographers, as well as on the extent to which pornography respects our capacity to engage in democratic debate. Whether it does depends upon the message it conveys. As we saw earlier, even the message that women are subordinate to men is protected political speech according to US courts, though the Antipornography Civil Rights Ordinance regarded women's submission to male domination as a violation of women's civil rights. Viewing women as inferior to men certainly is a political message, however wrong and distasteful, and one relevant to much political debate on reproductive freedom, for example, or on family and employment law. What, then, is its relationship with the democratic argument for free speech?

Women have an interest equal to that of men in being able to participate fully in political debate and democratic life. If women live in a society in which they are considered inferior to men, and if pornography contributes to creating this inequality, then it seems that pornography has significant anti-democratic implications. The argument that pornography *silences* women (see p. 121) is highly relevant here. If women are reluctant to speak out, if their authority is undermined, or if they are misunderstood (West 2018), this greatly impedes their contribution to democratic debate.

In summary, while there is a sense in which pornography could be said to contribute to democratic debate, allowing its widespread production, distribution and consumption may be too high a price to pay for this contribution, if pornography reinforces gender inequality and therefore democratic inequality in the public domain.

6
Contemporary Challenges

Introduction

We have sought in this book to survey long-standing and recent issues surrounding free speech, many of which have been revivified by current-day developments such as online hate, Internet pornography, religious resurgence and populist politics. In a short book like this we cannot analyse every relevant topic comprehensively or even in depth, not least because free speech considerations play a role in so many emerging political debates. Nonetheless, in this final chapter we provide a flavour of three of these debates: controversial figures no-platformed by university students as part of the new practice of cancel culture; the phenomenon of fake news in democratic societies; and the use of social media to shame individuals deemed guilty of violations of common norms. Our aim is to illustrate both the normative complexity that underlies the heat and noise generated by these issues and the continuing relevance of looking at free speech through the lenses of truth, autonomy and democracy.

No-platforming and free speech

Universities have often been hotbeds of political controversy, but in recent years issues of free speech have been at the apex of campus debate. In part this reflects ideological battles between left and right carried out on campus, recently augmented by 'culture wars' and identity politics, and presently fuelled by the rise of online debates and social media. Whatever the causes, the last few years have seen the rise of a distinct new vocabulary in which free speech is pitted against protecting students from various kinds of harms. Some of these debates have involved faculty members whose teaching runs against the grain of students' (or simply mainstream) political views, or who teach topics or use terms with which students feel uncomfortable (or worse). This state of things has elicited the notion of 'trigger warnings' and, from the opposite side, which is often the political right, the objection that today's students are 'snowflakes'. Students are said to require 'safe spaces', free from the possible encroachment of harmful views, or else 'free speech zones' where anything can be said.

In the present section we discuss just one aspect of this controversy: the policy of no-platforming, which bars controversial individuals from speaking on university campuses or sometimes rescinds their invitation to speak. The policy is not new in the United Kingdom: it was first adopted by the National Union of Students in the 1970s, to keep far-right parties and movements such as the National Front away from campus.[1] The range of persons who have been no-platformed extends nowadays to figures on the left as well as on the right of the political spectrum; academics, well-known personalities and individuals who enjoy some public prestige are among those affected. Some individuals are contentious because of the part they played in past injustices (e.g. Amber Rudd, disinvited from Oxford University as a consequence of her role in the Windrush controversy about the status of commonwealth immigrants to Britain),[2] or through association with other contentious persons (e.g. Ivanka Trump).[3] Professional provocateurs such as Milo Yiannopoulos, Katie Hopkins and Ben Shapiro have also been no-platformed. Some excluded individuals are effectively hate speakers; others have views that are offensive (if a line can be drawn between offensive and hate speech) or are considered unacceptable for other reasons, for example by a group of students. It is worth noting that, since extremist speakers thrive on controversy, no-platforming them can be made to appear a badge of honour, one that gives them more rather than less publicity.

That last point aside, what case can be made in defence of no-platforming? One argument is that university inquiry should be systematic, rigorous, impartial and evidence-based. Inducted into such norms of inquiry, students are better positioned to become critical thinkers, able to assess alternative viewpoints and take their place as independent citizens who contribute reasoned views to public deliberation. This is quite different from the marketplace of ideas in the public square, where, on a literal interpretation, free speech consumers could endorse any ideas, however abhorrent, prejudiced or ignorant. This 'community of inquiry' argument, as we shall call it, is defended by Robert Post (2017; cf. Fish 2019, pp. 68–72), who distinguishes sharply between free speech and public discourse: according to him, the latter includes the critical evaluation of ideas. Just as a professor appointed to teach mathematics could not legitimately complain if she were censured by university authorities for lecturing students on Donald Trump's failings, so too guest speakers may be sent away if they fail to respect the educative aims of public discourse. Post also points out that universities are schools of democratic citizenship and that speakers who are not committed to the basic norms of equal respect and civility that lie at the heart of this ideal can be legitimately excluded.

Robert Simpson and Amia Srinivasan (2018) build on Post's argument, emphasising how an academic faculty, made up as it is of disciplinary experts, legitimately exercises some control over the kinds of speech that characterise universities as institutions. Faculty members grade their students' work, set the curriculum, award doctorates, review one another's research, and make appointments on academic merit – all tasks guided by an ideal of the academy as the kind of institution that exercises content discrimination over what is said. In contrast to the public square, this environment demands *inequality* of status among ideas, since a university's purpose is to subject ideas to critical scrutiny and establish which ones are true and cogent and which ones are false and ill-founded.

Such disciplinary practices also enable universities to maintain some institutional independence from the potentially corruptive influence of external forces, for example commercial interests that seek to influence research results, or governments that wish to silence uncomfortable conclusions.

These considerations support the exclusion of speakers who would subvert the disciplinary independence of a university's intellectual life – that is, in our terms, its status as a community of inquiry. Just as it is acceptable to bar from teaching and public speaking faculty members who potentially deny the reality of the Holocaust or climate change, for example, so external speakers who espouse such views can be denied permission to address the members of a university, especially students, if they fail to respect that university's intellectual culture. By the same token, Simpson and Srinivasan point out, it would be wrong to no-platform credible speakers – for instance a right-wing economist opposed to social welfare policies, yet who grounds her work in solid scientific research – merely because their views are unwelcome or unacceptable to some students. Thus people whose work fails to meet academic norms, such as the discredited Holocaust denier David Irving, can be excluded from the ranks of potential speakers, whereas controversial yet genuine academics with sound standards of research should not be no-platformed.

One response to this argument distinguishes between the core research and teaching context of a university and broader public debate on campus. In more recent work, Simpson (2020) calls this response 'the standard view' of campus speech. It consists in differentiating a 'professional zone', the space where key educational and scholarly activities are conducted (lecture theatres, labs, etc.), from a more permissive, 'larger free speech zone' that, unlike the former, does not impose content discrimination over what is said and how it is expressed (Chemerinsky and Gillman 2017, p. 77; see also Shiffrin 2014, p. 213). Simpson (2020) rejects this distinction and argues that neither a Millian marketplace of ideas argument nor one that stresses the key role of universities in educating democratic citizens justifies unconstrained freedom of speech across campus. The former neglects the fact that universities 'should not adopt an uncritical stance toward work which demonstrates ignorance or incompetence relative to the local disciplinary standards' (p. 306). The latter overlooks the distinctive way in which universities should produce good democratic citizens, namely by 'fostering not only a culture of respect for dissenting opinions but also a sense that the value of dissent hinges on its being intelligent, coherent, and evidentially supported' (p. 312). On Simpson's view,

> the communicative climate of the campus at large is characterised by similar kinds of rigour, thoughtfulness, and deference to academic expertise as the lecture theatre or faculty research seminar. People are expected to comport themselves in a way that befits their being participants in a serious project of collective inquiry, and – as is already the case in formal teaching and research settings – this imposes standards on how they communicate with each other, and in various ways, on the actual substance of what they communicate. People ... who have repeatedly demonstrated a conspiratorial hostility to those standards, or who have otherwise revealed themselves to be unwilling to abide by them, aren't handed valuable speaking platforms. The university is still a place for vigorous debate and disagreement. But the style and temper of disagreement is quite unlike debate in public discourse, not just in the sense of being more mannerly, but in being more earnest about the actual aims of inquiry, and hence rising above mere altercation. (Simpson 2020, p. 299)

Neil Levy (2019) reaches a similar conclusion by emphasising the epistemic authority enjoyed by public figures invited to speak on university campuses. Such invitations are usually a sign of prestige; they certify that a speaker has some particular expertise in her area. Speaker invitations serve as 'higher-order evidence' of that expertise; they credentialise a speaker's status, suggesting that we should take her views seriously when we are often not authorities on an issue ourselves. Of course, students may interrogate a speaker's position but, lacking expert knowledge and being critical reasoners in the making, there will be limits to their ability to do so. Much epistemic authority is therefore taken on trust. In Levy's view, would-be invitees may legitimately be no-platformed if they undermine the principle of epistemic authority that lies at the heart of the ideal of a university. This would apply to Holocaust deniers, avowed racists, and those who reject the science of climate change.

Mill's truth-based defence of free speech – which is criticised for conceiving of society's public conversation as an intellectual seminar – seems apposite in this context. Considered as a community of inquiry, a university describes just those norms that must be in place for the success of the project of determining what is cogent and justified or, conversely, ill-founded. Yet there is an important difference. While Mill insisted on the liberty to espouse wrong-headed views as part of our quest to discover the truth, the argument we are looking at says that it is legitimate to exclude speakers whose opinions are false, pernicious, inflammatory or without proper, appropriate grounds. When we discussed Holocaust denial in Chapter 3 we considered this view, suggesting that wrong-headed views can be disallowed, especially in disciplines where there are undisputed matters of fact. But, in the case of much university inquiry, this will not apply. The best way of aligning the community of inquiry argument with Mill's view is to emphasise the deliberative interpretation of the latter. According to this interpretation, what extremist speakers fail to observe is the intellectual virtues of open-minded inquiry, argumentative rigour, responsiveness to evidence, and so on; and *this* is what justifies the exclusion of such speakers.

As far as autonomy is concerned, the community of inquiry argument is redolent of the debate on hate speech. Speaker autonomy can be marshalled against a blanket ban on contentious viewpoints. Listener autonomy suggests that students should have the opportunity to consider all viewpoints. As we have seen, however, some kinds of speech can bypass or, worse still, actively undermine autonomy. Such speech makes it less likely that its listeners will arrive at conclusions on the balance of reasons. This objection seems particularly apposite in view of the double fact that, when students encounter extremist positions, their capacity to scrutinise and evaluate alternative viewpoints is still in the making and universities are meant to develop precisely their capacity for autonomy. The case for no-platforming is therefore connected to the duties associated with cultivating autonomy.

How about the democracy argument for free speech? On the one hand, universities are by definition exclusionary; their meritocratic ideal of scholarly inquiry does not befit everyone. This attribute distinguishes them from the rest of the public square, which is more inclusive and egalitarian but where debate can be more uncivil, robust, ill-informed and offensive, even hateful. This is to draw a sharp distinction between communities of inquiry and the public square at large. On the other hand, if we conceptualise debate in the public square in more deliberative terms, as we suggested in Chapter 1, the community of inquiry argument seems to acquire relevance. On such a view, universities exemplify the rational deliberation that, as democrats hope, will characterise the public sphere; and the role of universities is to educate the next generation of citizens, empowering them to participate in those debates (see Simpson 2020, pp. 310–15). This second view seems to provide stronger democratic grounds for no-platforming than does the earlier view.

This position could appear to be elitist, just as Mill's does. It seems to prioritise refined academic speech, downgrading speakers who do not meet this standard. One may reply that all citizens, if well informed and sufficiently educated (even if not beyond school level), have some capacity for critical deliberation and some degree of responsiveness to evidence. Moreover, just as an effective deliberative democratic debate should incorporate many voices, which represent different interests, identities and social locations, so universities must encompass diverse perspectives – black and minority ethnic ones, for example – for their role as communities of inquiry not to be partisan and one-sided. Added to this is a duty of social justice: universities should reach out to less privileged individuals, who can benefit from the education they offer.

Another charge is that the democratic argument is too broad. After all, universities invite public figures from all walks of life – businesspeople, social activists, politicians, philanthropists – and usually the speech of such people will not attain the high standards of rigorous argumentation that characterise academic inquiry. It seems counterintuitive to no-platform the many public figures whose presence can enrich university life. On what grounds, then, is it possible to authorise these speakers, but veto the extremists? One way to respond is by distinguishing between external speakers who augment the campus experience and respect a university's core purpose as a community of inquiry even if they do not further it, and speakers who attack that core purpose by violating the canons of academic discourse: they invent facts, caricature arguments, misrepresent their opponents, replace reason with rhetoric, and so on. These considerations would not apply to contentious speakers such as Christine Lagarde or Condoleezza Rice, both of whom were no-platformed because they were seen as too right-wing (Garton Ash 2016, pp. 15–18). More troublesome are writers whose views are widely discredited on academic grounds or regarded as unacceptable – for instance the American political scientist Charles Murray, whose views on intelligence, race and welfare are regarded as racist by many.[4]

It is noteworthy that the community of inquiry argument bypasses – even if it does not reject – the main reason that advocates of no-platforming appeal to, namely that such a policy prevents certain individuals from inflicting harm on students and other people on campus. What can be said for this line of defence?

Here we revisit the terrain of hate speech, as discussed in Chapter 2, and the idea of civic subordination at its core. More specifically, some extremist speakers (e.g. far-right politicians) seem to meet the criteria for hate speech: they stigmatise certain groups of students, defame them by spreading malicious or damaging statements, rob them of dignity, incite hatred, or contribute to a climate of fear and insecurity on campus. On the view we are examining here, no-platforming could be understood as a performative means of asserting the dignity, rights and standing of those groups that it is anticipated extremist speakers would attack. It expresses a university's commitment to its members' equal dignity, rights and standing. Further, no-platforming prevents the occurrence, on campus, of particular instances of harm to vulnerable ethnic, religious and other minorities that could be reasonably predicted in the absence of such a policy.

One issue with the harm argument is that whether or not some group is harmed depends upon one's political commitments, but in many cases these are contested. This could apply to Germaine Greer and other prominent figures accused of transphobia, for example (Simpson and Srinivasan 2018). In such cases, whose view should we defer to? Moreover, given that the point of a free speech principle is that some harm may be permitted in the interests of free speech, we need to determine both the magnitude and the likelihood of the permissible harm. This issue of harm also raises questions of moral responsibility and empirical causation (cf. Simpson and Srinivasan 2018). As we saw in Chapter 2, it is not always easy to connect specific instances of hate speech to the harm it is said to cause.

If these sorts of issues can be resolved, then perhaps avoiding harm offers another defence of no-platforming, alongside the community of inquiry argument. That defence will always be controversial and a matter of applying one's judgement to specific contexts. Our purpose has simply been to sketch how the policy *may* be defended. There are other ways for students and other categories of people to express their opposition to invited speakers with controversial or extremist ideas. These include demonstrations, marches, campaigns and other forms of counterspeech, meetings designed to air student grievances, civil disruptions, and so on. These need not be alternatives to no-platforming, but in many instances they are more appropriate, for pragmatic or for principled reasons, if one rejects no-platforming altogether.

Fake news and free speech

In 2016, a pizza parlour in Washington, DC became the centre of a conspiracy theory about Hillary Clinton and other prominent Democrats. According to rumours widely circulated via social media, Clinton and her fellow partisans were running a child sex trafficking ring and using the pizza parlour in question as one of the key hubs. The conspiracy theory was eventually debunked (Rini 2017, p. E48; see also Goldman 2016). More recently, amid the COVID-19 crisis, '[a] WhatsApp message in Arabic says that if you have the circular scar from the jab on your arm [from the tuberculosis BCG vaccine], you could be "75% protected" against Covid-19',[5] a claim discredited by the World Health Organization (WHO).[6] These are only two out of countless instances of fake news, a global phenomenon that has become prominent over the past few years, especially since the Brexit referendum in the United Kingdom and the 2016 and 2020 presidential elections in the United States.

Cases such as these should trouble any citizen concerned about truth, democracy and the public interest, especially when large numbers of people – over two thirds in the United States according to one study (see Chambers 2020, p. 3) – get their news from social media. Here we analyse the phenomenon of fake news more narrowly, from the perspective of free speech. While a simple construal of free speech gives citizens the right to express any opinion, even if it is clearly false, the spread of fake news can erode others' speech by undermining the values that their speech serves – or so we suggest. First, though, we will survey briefly a number of ways in which the phenomenon has been defined in the modest number of philosophical discussions devoted to it.

One definition comes from Gelfert, who categorises fake news as 'the deliberate presentation of (typically) false or misleading claims as news, where the claims are misleading *by design*' (Gelfert 2018, pp. 85–6). Regina Rini adds to this definition by describing the goals of those who spread fake news:

> A fake news story is one that purports to describe events in the real world, typically by mimicking the conventions of traditional media reportage, yet is known by its creators to be significantly false, and is transmitted with the two goals of being widely re-transmitted and of deceiving at least some of its audience. (Rini 2017, p. E45)

Aikin and Talisse (2018) similarly emphasise the mimicry of journalistic conventions and hint at its harmfulness:

Fake news characterizes the activities of institutions that *pose* as journalistic which by design feed and codify the *antecedent* biases of a pre-selected audience by exploiting their vulnerabilities (cognitive and otherwise), all with a view towards facilitating some decidedly political objective.

These definitions highlight in the first place the importance of intentions in fake news: those who generate it deliberately attempt to mislead people. Second, they emphasise how fake news is presented in a way that appears to employ standard journalistic methods, even though it does not. These seem to be the two key features of fake news, while other features are not essential. For example, while political goals are often central to the motives of fake news originators, this is not always the case; sometimes the goal of fake news production is financial gain (Rini 2017, p. E45). Likewise, while fake news often exploits people's cognitive vulnerabilities, sometimes evidence about the latter is uncertain (Chambers 2020, p. 12); the effectiveness of fake news may be the result of flawed institutional structures rather than the result of individual epistemic or cognitive shortcomings (Rini 2017).

With these two complementary definitions to hand, how should we understand fake news from a theoretical perspective? Does it inevitably impede the goals of free speech, or can it sometimes contribute to them? Given that fake news is about information that is not true, an obvious starting point is the consequentialist argument from truth. The fact that fake news is deliberately false but presented as a contribution to the truth seems to suggest that it inherently undermines the discovery of truth. As we know, however, Mill believed that allowing false views helps to reinforce true ones by ensuring that we hold the latter in a more informed, lively way, on the basis of reason and evidence rather than as dead dogma; moreover, false opinions may contain some partial truth. Mill believed that truth should win out in open debate and that, over time, free speech would ensure that false opinions are gradually eradicated from the public sphere, as people are presented with the relevant facts and arguments. Yet when it comes to fake news these assumptions are problematic.

Mill assumes that the discovery of truth is a broadly desirable goal. But the increasingly academically credible idea of 'post-truth' 'suggests that ... people do not really care that much about the truth or they care about other things (partisan causes) more than the truth' (Chambers 2020, p. 2; cf. Fish 2019, pp. 170–4). 'Post-truth ... postulates that, with an increase in the number and political effectiveness of falsehoods entering the public sphere, one sees a decrease in the salience of truth or objective facts in opinion and will-formation' (Chambers 2020, p. 4). Mill assumes that truth is a constituent of well-being, but it might have increasingly less weight in contemporary societies by comparison with factors such as advancing one's partisan goals, or group solidarity.

We observed in our discussion of Holocaust denial that allowing the expression of false opinions may in fact contribute to their widespread endorsement. This is the exact opposite of Mill's assumption that we are primed for truth. We noted how, according to Schauer (2012, p. 137), this process may be affected by such factors as the style and charisma of speakers, the predisposition of listeners, and the frequency with which false views are presented. In the case of fake news in the new media environment, the same basic syndrome is amplified for at least three important reasons: psychological, ethical and institutional.

As for the psychological reasons, people may be prone to believe false information owing to various cognitive biases that fake news sources tend to exploit. These include confirmation bias (we prefer information that is in line with our existing beliefs; see Gelfert 2018, p. 111), repetition effects (being repeatedly exposed to the same information renders it more persuasive in our eyes; see Gelfert 2018, p. 112), and motivated reasoning (we want to win arguments rather than discover the truth; see Chambers 2020, p. 11).

Relatedly, people may be inclined to believe fake news owing to the absence of what Simone Chambers, borrowing from Bernard Williams, calls the virtue of 'accuracy'. This is an ethical rather than epistemic virtue, which entails 'making a goodwill effort and to find out what is true or to acquire true belief' (Chambers 2020, p. 13). Accuracy is significant because we all suffer from cognitive biases, and it is important in a democratic public sphere where all citizens are consumers of news and have a political say.

A final factor is today's social media infrastructure, which allows fake news to diffuse so rapidly. Rini (2017) suggests that this infrastructure is characterised by unstable norms about message sharing. Take for example the now customary proviso 'a retweet is not an endorsement', which many Twitter users include in their profile description. As Rini points out, 'many of us implicitly assume that our social media interlocutors *do believe* what they share, even though we are vaguely aware they may later disclaim it. This is part of what makes social media testimony aberrant' (p. E48, emphasis added). When many people, on the basis of this assumption, begin to share or even like a fake news story, this may lead to a 'tragedy of the epistemic commons' (p. E44):

> when all [these individual communicative acts] appear summed together, this ambiguity seems to wash away. Perhaps the implicit thought is like this: could it really be that *all* these people aren't *really* testifying to this? A thought like that might overwhelm ordinary skepticism about ridiculous testimony. (Rini 2017, p. E49)

People tend to join like-minded others on social media, and to trust and believe them because of their shared values. This 'epistemic partisanship' is generally reasonable in a non-ideal world, since we do not have the time to check all our sources of information all the time (pp. E50–E54). However, epistemic partisanship is problematic in social media settings, with their rapid and widespread diffusion of messages, since it reduces the inclination to verify our sources by sifting the factual evidence and by looking at various other factors, for example the motivation of those who supply that evidence.

In sum, the phenomenon of fake news challenges all the basic constituents of Mill's truth-based argument for free speech: we are not always equipped to recognise truth, nor do we necessarily care if we do; we do not live in an environment conducive to truth, and we cannot assume that true and accurate views will drive out false and misleading ones. This also highlights the issue of the take-up of free speech. Being affected by personal and institutional biases, some people's speech will have a much harder time being accepted by others if it challenges group prejudices or common stereotypes, or simply if it is presented by less trusted groups – itself an effect of fake news. Thus fake news reduces the credibility of some agents in the economy of truth, as well as devaluing truth's currency in general.

Similar considerations affect the autonomy argument for free speech as well. Being subject to multiple biases and ethical limits, we are not as autonomous as we like to believe (Moles 2007). Free speech is invariably not the outcome of our autonomous powers and, contrary to Scanlon's optimistic assumptions, we rarely decide on the balance of reasons. This is at least what fake news suggests.

It could be argued that fake news, if used to advance an important political cause or message, makes a contribution to public debate, and therefore to free speech as conceptualised by the argument from democracy. As we saw in our discussion of Holocaust denial, some courts have considered permissible the use of false information (e.g. false statistics about animal cruelty) in advancing a good cause (e.g. the promotion of animal welfare and animal rights). Likewise, one could argue that fake news stories, while hindering truth discovery, advance democratic debate by rendering an audience disposed to listen to the fundamental moral or political arguments that their advocates want to communicate.

In the case of animal cruelty, however, there is an underlying moral issue advanced by those with sincere beliefs: the scale of cruelty is exaggerated, but that exaggeration is intended to induce critical reflection. In the case of fake news, such purposes are absent; the motives of those who create it are usually sinister, not benign, and its effect is to stymie rather than stimulate reasoned discussion. It is hardly surprising, then, that widespread fake news undermines people's trust in the democratic process (Chambers 2020, p. 9). This matters especially if one adopts not a majoritarian but a deliberative model whereby democracy has 'truth-tracking potential' (p. 8): what we take to be true – or, perhaps better, what we take to be well founded or convincing – *is* what emerges from open, unforced deliberation, in which everyone has a say.

Fake news is profoundly disruptive to this process. If it insinuates itself into citizens' views, it undermines democracy's function of vindicating claims to truth; it diminishes citizens' trust that deliberation will arrive at the most cogent views; and, as fake news is generally purveyed by a small minority for its own ends, it is antithetical to democracy's credentials of being egalitarian, inclusive, and a means by which all citizens can raise claims that reflect their own experience during public deliberation (p. 9).

How, then, could we combat fake news, or diminish its influence? One method that seems consistent with deliberative democracy's truth-discerning function is counterspeech: declaiming the truth against lies and misinformation. Yet fake news utterances can shift the conversational norms on a given topic; this is what Lepoutre (2019, p. 158) calls the 'stickiness of ignorant speech'. For example, when, before the 2016 Brexit referendum, the Leave campaign used a message on a red bus to say that the United Kingdom was sending £350 million every week to the EU that could have been diverted to fund the NHS, the Remain campaign tried to counter the claim by pointing out that the figure was exaggerated. Yet this action, paradoxically, reinforced the salience of the misleading message. Moreover, even if successful, counterspeech may be insufficient to undo the harm to the democratic process, including the election of 'dangerous policies and candidates' (p. 165) whose flaws have remained concealed as a result of political misinformation,

Lepoutre (2019) recommends instead a pre-emptive rather than a retroactive form of counterspeech, one that aims at undermining fake news and other types of harmful speech *before* they begin to circulate within the public sphere and shift the conversational norms (p. 180). This kind of counterspeech includes disseminating politically relevant information that will help citizens to assess fake news stories more critically, and warning audiences about the unreliability of fake news sources before they produce the fake news (or even as they continue to produce it). This may be idealistic in a post-truth era, when all sources of information are regarded as partisan, but augmenting individuals' cognitive resistance to fake news is clearly important.

In a similar vein, Rini argues that we should embrace

'a norm that denies "a retweet is not an endorsement". People who share news should be unambiguously understood to lend their testimonial endorsement (barring explicit disclaimer), and should be held accountable if their claims are later shown false, in just the same way that a person spreading false rumors about an acquaintance may be held accountable' (Rini 2017, p. E55). Further, she suggests that stories that prove to be fake news after fact checking should be flagged by social media platforms – as indeed Twitter is now doing – and individual social media users who have repeatedly shared such stories be assigned a stigmatising low 'reputation score', thus having their authority undermined in the eyes of other users.

One could argue that regulating fake news is a violation of the rights and interests of speakers (see Rini 2017, p. E56). But, as we have seen in the case of the democratic argument in particular, regulation can serve free speech values. In her book *On Lying, Morality, and the Law*, Shiffrin (2014, p. 118) maintains that 'legal regulation of lies need not offend the important values protected by freedom of speech and, in particular by the free speech traditions articulated within [the] First Amendment'. The First Amendment bars limiting speech on the basis of content discrimination; but, if we regulate lies, this is because of concerns about the sincerity of the speaker, not about the substance of their message. If producers of fake news know that it is false, they can be censured in accordance with content neutrality. There remain nonetheless pragmatic reasons for not regulating fake news, namely to prevent possible government abuse (a fourth justification for free speech we mentioned in Chapter 1).

As fake news is, unfortunately, poised to become increasingly salient in public discourse, it is probable that scholarly discussion of it will become an ever more important part of the debate on free speech.

Online public shaming and free speech

Public shaming is another example of an area in which people *act* with speech, hence an area in which speech requires further normative investigation. It is also a phenomenon where harm arises because of the sum of many voices – an aggregative harm reflecting the great volume of speech. That public opinion has the power to harm is not new, of course. Mill was quite aware of it in *On Liberty*, where he highlights how social sanctions may be as effective as legal ones in responding to those who merit criticism. At the same time, Mill was acutely aware of the dangers of the tyranny of public opinion and of how it could stifle individuality and experiments in living. Both these perspectives are relevant to public shaming today.

Online shaming involves cases where individuals are widely and publicly criticised on social media for some comment or action of theirs that, according to their attackers, represents a serious failing of some kind. The quick pace of communications on social media means that initial tweets, posts or other messages have a multiplier effect, swiftly cascading to a crescendo of outrage against which the individual target, culpable or not, is relatively powerless. As a public form of social sanction that leaves individuals vulnerable to the gaze of others, if not humiliated, online shaming looks similar to the practice of shaming punishments – for instance when the identities and pictures of shoplifters or other thieves are publicly displayed for the whole community to see.

Is this an appropriate form of free speech? Perhaps it is, when the norms an individual violates guard against racist or sexist behaviour. Thus, in 2013, the communications executive Justine Sacco was targeted by a myriad of shaming messages after tweeting "Going to Africa. Hope I don't get AIDS. Just kidding. I'm white!" while travelling from New York to Cape Town (Billingham and Parr 2020a, p. 112; 2020b, p. 372). As a result, Sacco was fired by her employer while still on the plane, without having the opportunity to offer an explanation for her tweet or apologise. In fact, as a South African herself, Sacco claimed that she was parodying the racist attitudes of her white compatriots. But online public shaming is not restricted to targeting racist or sexist speech. The American dentist Walter Palmer, for example, was widely criticised after he shot a much loved lion in Zimbabwe, even though he had obtained the necessary permits.[7]

The incidence or rate of occurrence of online public

shaming increased during the COVID-19 pandemic, as individuals became the target of online accusations, insults and threats on account of their alleged infringement of restrictive government measures. For example, in March 2020, at the height of the COVID-19 crisis, CBS News circulated via Twitter a video of American students partying and getting drunk during their spring break in Miami, blatantly ignoring social distancing guidelines and making statements such as 'If I get corona, I get corona.' Many Twitter users commented on the video, some of them using abusive language or asking hospitals not to treat these students should they contract COVID-19. In another case, a man from Tennessee became the target of many heated comments for having stockpiled 17,700 bottles of hand sanitiser in order to resell them at higher prices. As a result of that shaming campaign, the man apologised and gifted his stockpile to a local church.[8]

How might we navigate these kinds of cases, and what do they imply for free speech? According to Paul Billingham and Tom Parr (2020a, 2020b), online public shaming can play a positive role by informally enforcing social norms against various types of harmful action or speech. In general, informal social norms offer a potentially useful alternative to legal regulation, one more effective than self-censorship but not coercive in the way legal intervention is. Public shaming *communicates* the norm to the individual who has violated it, *deters* others from similar behaviour in the future, and *affirms* a community's shared adherence to the norm. However, as these examples illustrate, online public shaming can also have serious negative effects on its targets. Does this mean that this practice should always be condemned? Not necessarily. Billingham and Parr (2020a, pp. 5–10) develop a set of criteria designed to assess online public shaming and to indicate when it is permissible and when not.

The first criterion they propose is proportionality: the negative consequences of online public shaming should not exceed its positive outcomes. Shaming should be used only to enforce morally authoritative social norms (Billingham and Parr 2020a, 2020b), and these should encompass more than just norms that condemn sexism and racism; for example civic norms that enable peaceful cooperation between citizens, such as the practice of queueing or cleaning up one's pet's mess, should also fall under this category. Yet shaming has reputational and psychological costs for those whom it targets, costs that depend in part on the number of people who see it and share it. Relevant to proportionality is also the seriousness of the harm that the norm violator has inflicted and how liable she is for her actions (Billingham and Parr 2020a, pp. 5–7). By preventing her from giving an explanation or from apologising for her conduct, for example, the shaming penalties inflicted on Justine Sacco look disproportionate. A second criterion is necessity: the communicative, deterrent and expressive functions of shaming must be no more harmful than any alternative means of encouraging norm compliance. Third, shaming must respect violators' privacy by not disclosing irrelevant or highly sensitive information about them. Fourth, public shaming must not threaten, disparage or abuse the violator, or attack her on the basis of arbitrary factors such as her race or gender, or amount to character assassination. Finally, it must seek as far as possible to reintegrate the violator into the community rather than permanently stigmatising her as an outcast. It should not impede her participation in public debate.

These are demanding criteria and the decentralised and fast-paced world of online messaging in particular means that very often they will not be met, though Billingham and Parr (2020a, pp. 14–15) mention some instances where they have all been satisfied, for instance when a scholar was constructively shamed for including sexist and homophobic passages in an academic paper. The chances of meeting the criteria can be augmented through measures that seek to hold the wrongdoers accountable for their norm infringement and encourage the shamers to appeal to broadly accepted communal standards, not to their personal interests and emotions. Accountability, the authors claim, can be increased by reducing the opportunities for anonymity online. Although allowing anonymous speech can result in a more diverse public forum, the tension between anonymity and accountability is evident (Barendt 2016).

By contrast, Guy Aitchison and Saladin Meckled-Garcia (2020) interpret online public shaming as a form of informal punishment that inflicts severe penalties on its victims.

Those who use social media to criticise individuals for having violated common norms and codes are, they argue, attempting to impose on them a reputational penalty in the name of the moral community. Since that penalty has a stigmatising character, it carries a message of ostracism: those subjected to online shaming are effectively being told that they are excluded from the community of norm-respecting citizens. This, by itself, makes it harder for them to exercise freedom of speech in stating their own point of view, especially if they come from an already vulnerable group. Worse still, the relatively anarchic nature of social media means that there is no check on the escalation of shame; it all depends on how widespread the knowledge of a person's 'crime' turns out to be and how many choose to criticise it. Many of these individuals probably know little of the context or the details of the original case, so their comments can easily be overstated or inaccurate.

The point of the punishment analogy, for Aitchison and Meckled-Garcia, is to draw attention to the lack of due process in the practice of online public shaming. There is for example no automatic right of reply. Unless accountability norms of the kind Billingham and Parr recommend emerge, this feature of punishment is absent too. Shaming is also disrespectful, since shamers are effectively punishing a person for choices she has made that, albeit criticisable, are legally and perhaps morally permissible. Certainly this observation applies to all the examples we gave above, including those of controversial speech. There is also a difference between inviting a person to feel shame and to reflect upon an action of hers that transgresses a norm or a rule and collectively tarring her with the brush of stigma. Also, there is no formal check or procedure for judging which norms exactly are policed by the denizens of social media; and this is another indication of the lack of due process. After all, norms are often contested. In another case, the academic Steven Salaita had a job offer at the University of Illinois withdrawn after the social media reaction to a series of tweets he had made that were critical of Israel (Fish 2019, pp. 94–7).

It is not entirely clear, however, whether online public shaming can reasonably be seen as a form of punishment, as opposed to vigorous criticism. Even as an informal practice, punishment must plausibly involve the authoritative censure of an individual for some violation she is deemed to have committed. But in the case of online shaming, while participants certainly mean to condemn the norm violator, it is less clear that they have the necessary authority to administer punishment, except in the loosest informal sense (to which due process and allied criteria of punishment do not generally apply).

The basic criticism remains, however, that shaming imposes a severe cost on those subjected to it. The message of ostracism may be accompanied by tangible severing of ties, as the shamed person feels obliged to resign from professional positions or is forced to leave. The British scientist Sir Tim Hunt was forced to resign from several research positions after making sexist comments in a speech delivered in South Korea.[9] Steven Salaita resigned from academia and works as a school bus driver.[10]

Shaming penalties remain controversial because of the public humiliation they seem to attract, even when the kinds of constraints Billingham and Parr recommend are present. Advocates maintain that these penalties serve to confront the offender with his offence, encourage the repentance necessary for him or her to be readmitted into the community of law-respecting citizens, and confirm the shared values that underlie the law. Critics such as the philosopher Martha Nussbaum (2015) argue that the stigmatisation they bring about is pernicious. Like Aitchison and Meckled-Garcia, Nussbaum sees in shaming penalties a failure to respect the equal dignity of convicted persons. Unlike guilt, which focuses on the wrongful act a person commits, shame has the person herself as its object; and shaming penalties denigrate persons, demoting them as lesser members of the political community, often provoking feelings of powerlessness and inadequacy, and undermining their self-worth.

Does online public shaming have any value as a form of free speech, despite its potentially harmful effects? To address that question, we turn for the last time to our three theories. We have interpreted the argument from truth as appealing to the stimulating effect that free speech often has on our capacities for critical reflection. But not all free speech has this effect. When it comes to online public shaming, there tends not to be much deliberation on the part of its perpetrators. The instantaneous nature of social media and the desire to be part of a short-lived movement encourage mere speech, rather than reasoned deliberation. However, if the effect of shaming is to encourage the targeted person to reflect on authoritative norms and rules, then perhaps online public shaming can help individuals to exchange falsehood for truth, to put it in Millian terms. People who abandon racist or sexist beliefs as a result of being shamed (or of having witnessed like-minded individuals being shamed) seem to undergo this kind of process. They may recant, just as the Tennessee man who donated his stockpile of hand sanitiser to the local church seemed to do.

When online public shaming silences those targeted by it, it may not only hinder the process of truth discovery but also undermine those people's autonomy. That is, the obvious, autonomy-based case for permitting online public shaming must be weighed against the practical impediments that those tainted by shaming will experience in exercising their autonomy as they try to present their side of the story. In the case of hate speech, victims can often find solidarity with fellow members of an oppressed group, as well as with members of the reasonable majority, and both kinds may embolden them in their efforts at counterspeech. Shamed persons, by contrast, may have fewer friends; the lack of relations marked by solidarity makes the exercise of autonomy harder. This is especially true if critics of shaming are correct when they observe that this practice penetrates our sense of identity and self-conception.

When it comes to the argument from democracy, advocates of online public shaming will maintain that the practice can play a key role in assisting citizens to hold politicians accountable. This seems to highlight an aspect that is perhaps not sufficiently explicit in Billingham and Parr's account. While they do recognise the existence of asymmetries of power, they highlight them mainly by comparing marginalised groups with relatively privileged ones (Billingham and Parr 2020a, p. 12 and 2020b, p. 382). But we should also draw a distinction between ordinary citizens on the one hand and politicians and public officials on the other. In particular, the key desiderata of proportionality and accountability that

Billingham and Parr argue for can perhaps be relaxed when the targets of online public shaming are members of the latter group. Just as anonymous political speech and whistle-blowing can be valuable (Barendt 2016) in spite of their perpetrators often being not very accountable, widespread anonymous online public shaming may be justified when it helps to hold those in positions of authority accountable to the general public. But here it is important to distinguish between a shaming process that is directed towards failures of political responsibility – as when a politician is shamed for showing indifference to victims in some major disaster – and the mobilisation of shame against some transgression in a politician's private life.

This is a taste of three current controversies on free speech. There are currently other controversies on this topic, and new ones can be guaranteed to emerge in the future for as long as humans are free to speak.

Conclusion

Freedom of speech, we often hear nowadays, is under attack, especially from those on the left, who in the past were the ones most apt and ready to defend it. According to those who describe this attack, controversial speakers are no-platformed by universities at the slightest whim of students who feel offended by their ideas. Lecturers with controversial views, or who teach works of literature or history with a racist message, are called out by students and university authorities, and sometimes lose their jobs. Statues associated with Britain's and other post-imperialist countries' colonial past, for instance the statue of the slave trader Edward Colston in Bristol, are torn down or made the subject of strenuous demands for their removal, as in the Rhodes Must Fall campaign at Oriel College, Oxford. Feminists who cast doubt on the reality of trans identities, such as J. K. Rowling, Germaine Greer and many others, are fiercely criticised as TERFs (trans-exclusionary radical feminists). News editors are censured or sacked for running controversial pieces, and journalists are barred from covering them. Books are withdrawn for their apparent inauthenticity on matters of race, gender or religion. TV shows with content possibly offensive to racial minorities are abruptly cancelled; past episodes are buried forever. Clumsy talk by leaders of organisations prompts a litany of complaints on Twitter, Facebook and other social media that call for them to be reprimanded.

University campuses in particular are at the forefront of this apparent movement. 'Snowflake' students today are said to take offence at the slightest provocation: they are angered by views they find unacceptable – especially views that challenge racial, ethnic, LGBTIQ+, religious and other identities – and swiftly call for retribution against their authors. Instead of a robust but civil debate, some argue, we have now a 'cancel culture', in which the new warriors of ideological orthodoxy seek to curtail or close down any speech they find objectionable.

Several fusillades published by those on the political right have made this charge in recent years. The libertarian online magazine *Spiked* has sustained a long campaign against the offence culture's 'safe spaces' and against 'wokeness' in universities in the United Kingdom.[1] A more thoughtful contribution, by Russell Blackford, who himself identifies as a liberal egalitarian, is *The Tyranny of Opinion* (2019). Blackford writes:

> It seems that more and more people, especially in younger generations, now support substantial legal and other formal restrictions on speech that they dislike. They can be very aggressive about this view, and some regard free speech advocacy as itself politically suspect. In this environment, free speech advocates, no matter how conscientious, well informed, cogent, and sympathetic to others they may be, can expect accusations of bigotry or secret agendas. At best, they'll be accused of insensitivity and cluelessness. (Blackford 2019, p. 78)

In the face of this manufacture of moral outrage, universities in the United Kingdom have been instructed to ensure that they maintain a robust free speech culture in return for government help after the COVID-19 pandemic,[2] while in the United States the receipt of federal research funding was contingent on universities proving they were not hostile to free speech and the First Amendment.[3]

It is unclear how far these charges genuinely describe the state of free speech in universities and elsewhere and how much they are a conservative, libertarian and populist confection.[4] Some scholars, drawing on empirical data, have disputed the scale of the phenomenon.[5] Anthony Leaker (2020) has argued that the vociferous defence of free speech by the political right, including white nationalists, has been a means to cloak further oppression of scapegoated ethnic and religious minorities, often genuinely harmed by their speech. Similarly, Gavan Titley maintains that 'invocations of free speech have become fundamental to reshaping how racism is expressed and legitimized in public culture … *free speech* has been adopted as a primary mechanism for validating, amplifying and reanimating racist ideas and racializing claims' (Titley 2020, pp. 11–12). We do not have the space to evaluate this counterview here, but to the extent that there has been a backlash against the (almost) unconstrained freedom of speech embraced by authors such as Ronald Dworkin (1981, 2009), C. Edwin Baker (1989, 1997, 2009), Eric Heinze (2016), Nadine Strossen (2018) and others, that is the context in which it needs to be understood.

It remains true, of course, that, in order to assert that another's speech should be constrained, regulated, censured, or even banned altogether – as opposed to being met with more speech – it is clearly insufficient to cite one's objections to it, state that its substance is unacceptable, or claim that one is offended. The harm, or even the profound offence (Feinberg 1985) that the speech in question causes needs to be articulated in a cogent and philosophically defensible way, so that the setback it causes to one's interests is clearly identified and explained. This is what we have surveyed in the pages of our book, explaining for instance Waldron's (2012) defence of hate speech laws, Rostbøll's (2009) autonomy-based analysis of the 'Danish cartoons', and Langton's (1990, 1993), Maitra's (2004, 2009, 2012) and McGowan's (2009) feminist critiques of pornography.

Free speech, we maintain, remains a fundamentally liberal value, whose rationale can be fully understood only from within the boundaries of the liberal tradition. Writers such as Feinberg, Waldron, Rostbøll and many others who argue for limits to free speech identify with liberalism; Langton, Maitra and McGowan, among other feminists, critical race theorists, old-style cultural conservatives, and communitarians are more sceptical of the liberal viewpoint or reject it altogether. Yet those who proclaim near-absolutist free speech against the 'cancel culture' claim to be liberals too – more precisely, *classical liberals* or *libertarians* (or new-style conservatives). Liberalism, however, is a capacious tradition, and it is *liberal egalitarianism* that has the conceptual and normative resources to acknowledge, evaluate and counteract the excesses of free speech – directed at racial and other minorities – in at least some instances. Most (though not all) academic liberals today are liberal egalitarians, and this is the tradition we identify with as authors of this book.

Liberalism's two fundamental values are freedom and equality, and much of the current debate on the alleged crisis of free speech has revolved around an understanding of free speech that is grounded in freedom; thus, when racist or sexist speakers are banned from university campuses, it is their freedom (and, more specifically, their negative freedom, i.e. freedom from interference) that it is being curtailed. But equality, understood not just as formal equality before the law but as substantive gender, racial and economic equality – the capacity of all people to chart their own course in life free from domination, oppression, subordination, lack of opportunity or, simply, penury – describes another important dimension of liberalism that should not be neglected.

The idea that these two values – freedom and equality – can conflict is hardly new. In the context of cancel culture and free speech, Teresa Bejan (2017) has traced it back to an analysis of the ancient Greek terms *isēgoria* ('equal right of speech') and *parrhēsia* ('outspokenness, candour, frankness'). While both are roughly translated into English as 'free speech', Bejan highlights their meanings and connotations, which are quite different from each other. *Isēgoria* can best be translated as 'equal speech in public' and refers to the equal right, enjoyed by citizens in ancient Athens, to take part in democratic public debate. Conversely, *parrhēsia* refers to the licence, or privilege, to speak truth to power without constraints, sometimes through offensive speech. Crucially, Bejan argues, both understandings of free speech have influenced liberalism today: the former via the European Enlightenment's emphasis on people's equal right to reasoned debate (which may exclude non-reasoned forms of speech such as hate speech), the latter through the influence of evangelicals and religious libertines on US free speech exceptionalism. Debates about campus speech, Bejan concludes, are not between defenders and critics of free speech, but rather between advocates of two *different* conceptions of free speech. Students who oppose racist or sexist speakers on campus do not reject free speech per se: they invoke 'the *equal right* to speech and equal access to a public forum in which the historically marginalized and excluded can be heard and count equally with the privileged' (Bejan 2017). This is a right that silencing forms of expression such as hate speech risk undermining. Addressing the crisis of free speech and liberalism requires combining *parrhēsia* and *isēgoria*.

Replenishing liberalism's capacity to defend the same effective rights of speech for all, whatever their identity or social background, demands eschewing libertarian excesses and placing equality alongside freedom at the forefront of a liberal defence of free speech. Much fascinating work in contemporary political theory has reflected carefully on what this implies, and much more should be said on this topic; but, for us, that is a project for another day.

Notes

Notes to Introduction

1 Visit https://twitter.com/jk_rowling/status/12693825183625093
  13?ref_src=twsrc%5Etfw%7Ctwcamp%5Etweetembed%7Ctw
  term%5E1269382518362509313%7Ctwgr%5Eshare_3&ref_
  url=https%3A%2F%2Fwww.nbcnews.com%2Ffeature%2
  Fnbc-out%2Fj-k-rowling-accused-transphobia-after-mocking-
  people-who-menstruate-n1227071.
2 Visit https://www.abc.net.au/news/2019-12-20/jk-rowling-back
  s-sacked-worker-in-transgender-speech-case/11817234.
3 Visit https://www.politico.com/news/2020/09/17/trump-black-li
  ves-matter-1619-project-417162.

Note to Chapter 1

1 Visit https://www.theguardian.com/uk-news/2020/apr/04/uk-ph
  one-masts-attacked-amid-5g-coronavirus-conspiracy-theory.

Notes to Chapter 2

1 Our definition is inspired by Jeremy Waldron's 2012 account of free speech, which we discuss later in the chapter.
2 Visit https://www.bbc.com/news/av/uk-34625512.
3 Visit https://www.bbc.com/news/uk-wales-south-east-wales-346 13148.
4 Visit https://www.nytimes.com/2020/06/18/world/europe/france -internet-hate-speech-regulation.html.
5 Visit https://www.gov.uk/government/consultations/online-harms-white-paper/online-harms-white-paper.
6 See the Supreme Court case *Virginia v Black* (2003).
7 Visit https://www.theguardian.com/us-news/2015/jun/16/donald-trump-announces-run-president.
8 In *Snyder v Phelps* (2011), the US Supreme Court ruled a tort for emotional distress to be unconstitutional in the case of a speech on the street on a matter of public concern. In the case in point the speech concerned the Westboro Baptist Church, which we mention briefly in the text that follows.
9 Visit https://www.theguardian.com/media/2015/apr/20/katie-ho pkins-sun-migrants-article-petition-nears-180000-mark.

Notes to Chapter 3

1 Visit https://www.independent.co.uk/news/uk/home-news/holoc aust-memorial-day-poll-uk-jews-murdered-nazi-germany-hope-not-hate-a8746741.html. It should be noted that the methodology used in this poll was criticised by the BBC statistics programme *More or Less*: https://www.bbc.co.uk/programmes/m00028cf.
2 Visit https://edition.cnn.com/interactive/2018/11/europe/antise mitism-poll-2018-intl.
3 Visit https://www.theguardian.com/world/2020/sep/16/holocau st-us-adults-study.
4 Visit https://www.theguardian.com/technology/2016/mar/30/mi crosoft-racist-sexist-chatbot-twitter-drugs.
5 Visit https://qz.com/646825/microsofts-ai-millennial-chatbot-be came-a-racist-jerk-after-less-than-a-day-on-twitter.
6 Visit https://www.theguardian.com/world/2020/aug/16/facebook-algorithm-found-to-actively-promote-holocaust-denial.

7   Facebook justified allowing Holocaust denial content on its pages by stating that their 'policies ... don't generally prohibit people from making statements about historical events, no matter how ignorant the statement or how awful the event' (https://www.jta.org/2011/07/28/global/facebook-firm-on-holocaust-denial-pages-despite-survivors-letter) and that they 'recognize people's right to be factually wrong about historic events' (https://ohpi.org.au/its-time-facebook-repents).

8   However, this policy will be replaced with one whereby those investigating the Holocaust and its denial will be directed to sources of 'credible information': visit https://www.bbc.co.uk/news/technology-54509975.

9   Visit https://www.theguardian.com/world/2020/aug/22/holocau st-denial-graffitied-at-site-of-nazi-massacre-in-france.

10 See, for example, https://www.bbc.co.uk/news/uk-england-der byshire-47230443.

11 Visit https://bleeckerstreetmedia.com/denial.

12 However, in 2012 France's Constitutional Council ruled that to extend the Gayssot Act to question the Armenian genocide was unconstitutional, as it violated freedom of speech. See the discussion at https://www.humanityinaction. org/knowledge_detail/memory-laws-in-france-and-their-impli-cations-institutionalizing-social-harmony.

13 Visit https://edition.cnn.com/2007/US/09/24/us.iran.

14 Visit https://www.reuters.com/article/us-racism-un-idUSLJ3498 0320090420.

15 Visit https://www.dailymail.co.uk/news/article-8571975/Holoc aust-survivors-urge-Facebook-remove-denial-posts.html.

16 Visit https://www.bbc.co.uk/news/uk-england-derbyshire-4723 0443.

Notes to Chapter 4

1   Visit e.g. https://www.bbc.com/news/magazine-19625542.

2   Visit e.g. https://www.fosters.com/news/20200117/guest-view-flag-burning-may-be-offensive-but-its-protected-free-speech.

3   Visit https://www.bbc.co.uk/news/uk-politics-45083275.

4   Visit https://www.bbc.co.uk/news/uk-politics-45083275.

5   Visit https://www.theguardian.com/media/2007/dec/05/indepen dentproductioncompanies.bbc.

6   Visit https://www.theguardian.com/media/2020/sep/01/charlie-hebdo-reprints-muhammad-cartoons-prophet-terror-trial.

7 Yet some might claim that it is morally problematic to be required to pay a licence fee in order to be able to watch certain TV channels that broadcast a few offensive programmes, when not paying the fee means not being able to watch any TV at all, as is the case with the BBC in the United Kingdom.

Notes to Chapter 5

1 Visit https://www.theguardian.com/commentisfree/2013/dec/21/ shunga-british-museum-japan-art-sex.
2 Visit https://www.theguardian.com/commentisfree/2013/dec/21/ shunga-british-museum-japan-art-sex.
3 To be fair to MacKinnon, her analysis of the causation involved is in other places in her work more nuanced and complex. See e.g. Eaton 2007, p. 696.
4 Visit https://freespeechdebate.com/discuss/privacy-free-speech- and-sexual-images-the-challenges-faced-by-legal-responses-to- revenge-porn.
5 The full text is available at http://www.nostatusquo.com/ACLU/ dworkin/other/ordinance/newday/AppD.htm.

Notes to Chapter 6

1 Visit https://www.nusconnect.org.uk/resources/nus-no-platform -policy-f22f.
2 Visit https://www.bbc.com/news/uk-england-oxfordshire-5176 8634.
3 Visit https://www.theguardian.com/us-news/2020/jun/06/ivanka -trump-cancel-culture-kansas-speech.
4 Visit https://www.politico.com/magazine/story/2017/05/28/ how-donald-trump-caused-the-middlebury-melee-215195.
5 Visit https://www.bbc.com/news/52310194.
6 Visit https://www.who.int/news-room/commentaries/detail/baci lle-calmette-gu%C3%A9rin-(bcg)-vaccination-and-covid-19.
7 Visit https://www.bbc.co.uk/news/world-us-canada-33710613.
8 These examples can be found at https://www.theguardian. com/science/2020/apr/04/pandemic-shaming-is-it-helping- us-keep-our-distance.

9 Visit https://www.theguardian.com/science/2015/jun/13/tim-hu
   nt-hung-out-to-dry-interview-mary-collins.
10 Visit https://www.chronicle.com/article/Ousted-From-Academe/
   245732.

Notes to Conclusion

1 Visit e.g. https://www.spiked-online.com/2020/07/24/wokeness-
   is-being-pushed-on-everyone.
2 Visit https://www.theguardian.com/education/2020/jul/16/engli
   sh-universities-must-prove-commitment-to-free-speech-for-
   bailouts.
3 Visit https://www.theguardian.com/us-news/2019/mar/21/trum
   p-college-university-free-speech-funding.
4 Visit https://www.theguardian.com/world/2019/sep/03/the-myt
   h-of-the-free-speech-crisis;   https://www.theguardian.com/news
   /2018/jul/26/the-free-speech-panic-censorship-how-the-
   right-concocted-a-crisis; and https://www.theguardian.com/com
   mentisfree/2020/feb/22/university-free-speech-crisis-censorship-
   enoch-powell.
5 Visit https://www.nbcnews.com/think/opinion/are-liberal-colleg
   e-students-creating-free-speech-crisis-not-according-ncna858906;
   https://www.vox.com/policy-and-politics/2018/8/3/17644180/
   political-correctness-free-speech-liberal-data-georgetown.

Bibliography

Abrams v United States, 250 US 616 (1919).

Aikin, S. F. and R. B. Talisse (2018). 'On "Fake News"', *3 Quarks Daily*, 21 May. https://www.3quarksdaily.com/3quarksdaily/2018/05/on-fake-news.html.

Aitchison, G. and S. Meckled-Garcia (2020). 'Against Online Public Shaming: Ethical Problems with Mass Social Media'. *Social Theory and Practice*.

American Booksellers Ass'n, Inc. v Hudnut, 771 F.2d 323 (7th Cir. 1985).

Bächtiger, A., J. D. Dryzek, J. Mansbridge and M. E. Warren (eds) (2018). *The Oxford Handbook of Deliberative Democracy* (Oxford: Oxford University Press).

Baker, C. E. (1989). *Human Liberty and Freedom of Speech* (New York: Oxford University Press).

Baker, C. E. (1997). 'Harm, Liberty and Free Speech'. *Southern California Law Review* 70(4): 979–1020.

Baker, C. E. (2009). 'Autonomy and Hate Speech', in I. Hare and J. Weinstein (eds), *Extreme Speech and Democracy* (Oxford: Oxford University Press), pp. 139–57.

Baker, C. E. (2011). 'Autonomy and Free Speech'. *Constitutional Commentary* 27(2): 251–80.

Barendt, E. M. (2005). *Freedom of Speech*, 2nd edn (Oxford: Oxford University Press).

Barendt, E. M. (2016). *Anonymous Speech: Literature, Law and Politics* (Oxford: Hart Publishing).

Beauharnais v Illinois, 343 US 250 (1952).

Bejan, T. M. (2017) 'The Two Clashing Meanings of "Free Speech"'. *Atlantic*, 2 December. https://www.theatlantic.com/politics/archive/2017/12/two-concepts-of-freedom-of-speech/546791.

Bell, D. (2020). 'Communitarianism', in E. N. Zalta (ed.), *The Stanford Encyclopedia of Philosophy*. https://plato.stanford.edu/entries/communitarianism.

Bhatti, G. K. (1984). *Behzti (Dishonour)* (London: Oberon Books).

Billingham, P. and T. Parr (2020a). 'Enforcing Social Norms: The Morality of Public Shaming'. *European Journal of Philosophy*. https://doi.org/10.1111/ejop.12543.

Billingham, P. and T. Parr (2020b). 'Online Public Shaming: Virtues and Vices'. *Journal of Social Philosophy* 51(3): 371–90.

Blackford, R. (2019). *The Tyranny of Opinion: Conformity and the Future of Liberalism* (London: Bloomsbury Academic).

Bonotti, M. (2015). 'Political Liberalism, Free Speech and Public Reason'. *European Journal of Political Theory* 14(2): 180–208.

Bonotti, M. and J. Seglow (2019). 'Self-Respect, Domination and Religiously Offensive Speech'. *Ethical Theory and Moral Practice* 22(3): 589–605.

Brandenburg v Ohio, 395 US 444 (1969).

Brettschneider, C. (2012). *When the State Speaks, What Should It Say? How Democracies Can Protect Expression and Promote Equality* (Princeton, NJ: Princeton University Press).

Brink, D. (2008). 'Mill's Liberal Principles and Freedom of Expression', in C. L. Ten (ed.), *Mill's On Liberty: A Critical Guide* (Cambridge: Cambridge University Press), pp. 40–61.

Brison, S. (1998). 'The Autonomy Defence of Free Speech'. *Ethics* 108(2): 312–39.

Brison, S. and K. Gelber (eds) (2019). *Free Speech in the Digital Age* (Oxford: Oxford University Press).

Brown, A. (2008). 'The Racial and Religious Hatred Act 2006: A Millian Response'. *Critical Review of International Social and Political Philosophy* 11(1): 1–24.

Brown, A. (2015). *Hate Speech Law: A Philosophical Examination* (New York: Routledge).

Brown, A. (2018). 'What Is So Special about Online (as Compared to Offline) Hate Speech?'. *Ethnicities* 18(3): 297–326.

Butz, A. (1976). *The Hoax of the Twentieth Century: The Case against the Presumed Extermination of European Jewry* (Richmond, Surrey: Historical Review Press).

Chambers, S. (2020). 'Truth, Deliberative Democracy, and the Virtues of Accuracy: Is Fake News Destroying the Public Sphere?'. *Political Studies* 68(4). https://doi.org/10.1177%2F0032321719890811.

Chaplinsky v New Hampshire, 315 US 568 (1942).

Chemerinsky, E. and H. Gillman (2017). *Free Speech on Campus* (New Haven, CT: Yale University Press).

Cohen v California, 403 US 15 (1971).

Cohen, J. (1993). 'Freedom of Expression'. *Philosophy and Public Affairs* 22(3): 207–63.

Cohen-Almagor, R. (2008). 'Hate in the Classroom: Free Expression, Holocaust Denial, and Liberal Education'. *American Journal of Education* 114(2): 215–41.

Cohen-Almagor, R (2015). *Confronting the Internet's Dark Side: Moral and Social Responsibility on the Free Highway* (Cambridge: Cambridge University Press).

Council of Europe (1953). *European Convention on Human Rights (ECHR)* [formally *Convention for the Protection of Human Rights and Fundamental Freedoms*]. Strasbourg. https://www.coe.int/en/web/conventions/full-list/-/conventions/treaty/005.

Council of the European Union (2007). 'Framework Decision on Combating Certain Forms and Expressions of Racism and Xenophobia by Means of Criminal Law'. https://eur-lex.europa.eu/legal-content/EN/TXT/?uri=LEGISSUM%3Al33178.

Davey, J. and J. Ebner (2019). '"The Great Replacement": The Violent Consequences of Mainstreamed Extremism'. Institute for Strategic Dialogue. https://www.isdglobal.org/wp-content/uploads/2019/07/The-Great-Replacement-The-Violent-Consequences-of-Mainstreamed-Extremism-by-ISD.pdf.

Delgado, R. (1982). 'Words That Wound: A Tort Action for Racial Insults, Epithets, and Name-Calling'. *Harvard Civil Rights–Civil Liberties Law Review* 17(1): 133–81.

Delgado, R. (1991). 'Campus Antiracism Rules: Constitutional Narratives in Collision'. *Northwestern University Law Review* 85(2): 343–87.

Delgado, R. and J. Stefancic (2014). 'Hate Speech in Cyberspace'. *Wake Forest Law Review* 49(2): 319–43.

Delgado, R. and J. Stefancic (1994). 'Cosmopolitanism inside out: International Norms and the Struggle for Civil Rights and Local Justice'. *Connecticut Law Review* 27(3): 773–88.

Devlin, P. (1968). *The Enforcement of Morals* (Oxford: Oxford University Press).

Dworkin, A. and C. MacKinnon (1983). 'Antipornography Civil Rights Ordinance'. http://www.nostatusquo.com/ACLU/dworkin/other/ordinance/newday/AppD.htm.

Dworkin, R. (1977). *Taking Rights Seriously* (Cambridge, MA: Harvard University Press).

Dworkin, R. (1981). 'Is There a Right to Pornography?'. *Oxford Journal of Legal Studies* 1(2): 177–212.

Dworkin, R. (1993). 'Women and Pornography'. *New York Review of Books*, 21 October.

Dworkin, R. (2009). 'Foreword', in I. Hare and J. Weinstein (eds), *Extreme Speech and Democracy* (Oxford: Oxford University Press), pp. v–ix.

Dyzenhaus, D. (1992). 'John Stuart Mill and the Harm of Pornography'. *Ethics* 102(3): 534–51.

Easton, S. (1994). *The Problem of Pornography: Regulation and the Right to Free Speech* (London: Routledge).

Easton, S. (1995). 'Autonomy and the Free Speech Principle', *Journal of Applied Philosophy* 12 (1): 27–39.

Eaton, A.W. (2007). 'A Sensible Antiporn Feminism'. *Ethics* 117(4): 674–715.

EEOC v Tyson Foods, Inc. (2006)

Estlund, D. (2008). *Democratic Authority: A Philosophical Framework* (Princeton, NJ: Princeton University Press).

Feinberg, J. (1985). *Offense to Others*, vol. 2 of *The Moral Limits of the Criminal Law* (Oxford: Oxford University Press).

Fish, S. (2019). *The First* (New York: Simon & Schuster).

Fricker, M. (2007). *Epistemic Injustice: Power and the Ethics of Knowing* (Oxford: Oxford University Press).

Garton Ash, T. (2016). *Free Speech: Ten Principles for a Connected World* (New Haven, CT: Yale University Press).

Gayssot Act (1990). 'Loi n° 90-615 du 13 juillet 1990 tendant à réprimer tout acte raciste, antisémite ou xénophobe'. Légifrance. https://www.legifrance.gouv.fr/affichTexte.do?cidTexte=JORFTE XT000000532990&dateTexte=&categorieLien=id.

Gelfert, Axel (2018). 'Fake News: A Definition'. *Informal Logic* 38(1): 84–117.

Gilmore, J. (2011). 'Expression as Realization: Speakers' Interests in Freedom of Speech'. *Law and Philosophy* 30(5): 517–39.

Goldman, Adam (2016). "The Comet Ping Pong Gunman Answers Our Reporter's Questions." *New York Times*, 7 December. https://www.nytimes.com/2016/12/07/us/edgar-welch-comet-pizza-fake-news.html.

Gray, J. (1996). *Mill on Liberty: A Defence* (London: Routledge).

Greenawalt, K. (1989). 'Free Speech Justifications'. *Columbia Law Review* 89(1): 118–55.

Grubbs, J. B., P. J. Wright, A. L. Braden, J. A. Wilt, and S. W. Kraus, (2019). 'Internet Pornography Use and Sexual Motivation: A Systematic Review and Integration'. *Annals of the International Communication Association* 43(2): 117–55.

Hald, G. H., N. M. Malamuth and C. Yuen (2010). 'Pornography and Attitudes Supporting Violence against Women: Revisiting the

Relationship in Nonexperimental Studies'. *Aggressive Behaviour* 36(1): 14–20.

Hare, I. (2009). 'Blasphemy and Incitement to Religious Hatred', in I. Hare and J. Weinstein (eds), *Extreme Speech and Democracy* (Oxford: Oxford University Press), pp. 289–310.

Hausman, D. M. and B. Welch (2010). 'Debate: To Nudge or Not to Nudge'. *Journal of Political Philosophy* 18(1): 123–36.

Haworth, A. (1998). *Free Speech* (London and New York: Routledge).

Heinze, E. (2016). *Hate Speech and Democratic Citizenship* (Oxford: Oxford University Press).

Heinze, E. (2018a). 'Karl Marx's Theory of Free Speech: Part 1', *Humanity*, 31 May. http://humanityjournal.org/blog/ karl-marxs-theory-of-free-speech-part-1.

Heinze, E. (2018b). 'Karl Marx's Theory of Free Speech: Part 2'. *Humanity*, 1 June. http://humanityjournal.org/blog/ karl-marxs-theory-of-free-speech-part-2.

Hornsby, J. and R. Langton (1998). 'Free Speech and Illocution'. *Legal Theory* 4(1): 21–37.

Howard, J. (2019). 'Free Speech and Hate Speech'. *Annual Review of Political Science* 22: 93–109.

Irving v Penguin Books Limited and Deborah E. Lipstat [sic] [2000] EWHC QB 115 (11 April 2000).

Irving, D. (1977). *Hitler's War* (New York: Viking Press).

Jones, P. (1980). 'Blasphemy, Offensiveness and Law'. *British Journal of Political Science* 10(2): 129–48.

Jones, P. (2011). 'Religion and Freedom of Expression: Is Offensiveness Really the Issue?'. *Res Publica* 17(1): 75–90.

Lægaard, S. (2007). 'The Cartoon Controversy: Offence, Identity, Oppression?'. *Political Studies* 55(3): 481–98.

Langton, R. (1990). 'Whose Right? Ronald Dworkin, Women, and Pornographers'. *Philosophy and Public Affairs* 19(4): 311–59.

Langton, R. (1993). 'Speech Acts and Unspeakable Acts'. *Philosophy and Public Affairs* 22(4): 293–330.

Langton, R. (2018). 'Blocking as Counterspeech', in D. Fogal, D. Harris and M. Moss (eds), *New Work on Speech Acts* (Oxford: Oxford University Press), pp. 144–62.

Lawrence, C. (1987). 'The Id, the Ego, and Equal Protection: Reckoning with Unconscious Racism'. *Stanford Law Review* 39(2): 317–88.

Leaker, A. (2020). *Against Free Speech* (London: Rowman & Littlefield).

Lepoutre, M. (2017). 'Hate Speech in Public Discourse: A Pessimistic Defense of Counterspeech'. *Social Theory and Practice* 43(4): 851–83.

Lepoutre, M. (2019). 'Can "More Speech" Counter Ignorant Speech?'. *Journal of Ethics and Social Philosophy* 16(3): 155–91.

Levy, N. (2019) 'No-Platforming and Higher-Order Evidence, or Anti-Anti-No-Platforming'. *Journal of the American Philosophical Association* 5(4): 1–16.

Lipstadt, D. (1994). *Denying the Holocaust: The Growing Assault on Truth and Memory* (London: Penguin Books).

MacIntyre, A. (1984). *After Virtue*, 2nd edn (Notre Dame, IN: University of Notre Dame Press).

MacKinnon, C. A. (1984). 'Not a Moral Issue'. *Yale Law & Policy Review* 2(2): 321–45.

MacKinnon, C. A. (1987). *Feminism Unmodified* (Cambridge, MA: Harvard University Press).

MacKinnon, C. A. (1992). 'Pornography, Civil Rights and Speech', in C. Itzin (ed.), *Pornography: Women, Violence and Civil Liberties* (Oxford: Oxford University Press), pp. 456–511.

MacKinnon, C. A. (1993). *Only Words* (Cambridge, MA: Harvard University Press).

MacKinnon, C. A. (2017). *Butterfly Politics* (Cambridge, MA: Belknap Press of Harvard University Press).

Maitra, I. (2004). 'Silence and Responsibility'. *Philosophical Perspectives* 18(1): 189–208.

Maitra, I. (2009). 'Silencing Speech'. *Canadian Journal of Philosophy* 39(2): 309–38.

Maitra, I. (2012). 'Subordinating Speech', in I. Maitra and M. McGowan (eds), *Speech and Harm: Controversies over Free Speech* (Oxford: Oxford University Press), pp. 94–120.

Mansbridge, J. and S. M. Okin (2007). 'Feminism', in R. Goodin, P. Pettit and T. Pogge (eds), *A Companion to Contemporary Political Theory*, 2nd edn (Oxford: Wiley Blackwell), pp. 332–59.

Margalit, A. and G. Motzkin (1996). 'The Uniqueness of the Holocaust'. *Philosophy and Public Affairs* 25(1): 65–83.

Mason, T. (1981). 'Intention and Explanation: A Current Controversy about the Interpretation of National Socialism', in G. Hirschfeld and L. Kettenacker (eds), *Der Führerstaat: Mythos und Realität* (Stuttgart: Klett-Cotta), pp. 21–40.

Matsuda, M. (1989). 'Public Response to Racist Speech: Considering the Victim's Story'. *Michigan Law Review* 87(8): 2320–81.

McGowan, M. K. (2009). 'Debate: On Silencing and Sexual Refusal'. *Journal of Political Philosophy* 17(4): 487–94.

McKinnon, C. (2006) *Toleration: A Critical Introduction* (London: Routledge).

McKinnon, C. (2007). 'Should We Tolerate Holocaust Denial?'. *Res Publica* 13(1): 9–28.

McTernan, E. (2018). 'Microaggressions, Equality, and Social Practices'. *Journal of Political Philosophy* 26(3): 261–81.

Meiklejohn, A. (1948). *Free Speech and Its Relation to Self-Government* (New York: Harper).

Mill, J. S. (1998) [1863]. 'Utilitarianism', in J. S. Mill, *On Liberty and Other Essays*, edited by John Gray (Oxford: Oxford University Press), pp. 131–204.

Mill, J. S. (2006) [1859]. *On Liberty and The Subjection of Women*, edited by A. Ryan (London: Penguin Books).

Miller v California, 413 US 15 (1973).

Moles, A. (2007) 'Autonomy, Free Speech and Automatic Behaviour'. *Res Publica* 13(1): 57–75.

New York Times Co. v Sullivan, 376 US 254 (1964).

Nussbaum, Martha (2015). *Hiding from Humanity: Disgust, Shame and the Law* (Princeton, NJ: Princeton University Press).

Parliament of the United Kingdom (1959). 'Obscene Publications Act'. http://www.legislation.gov.uk/ukpga/1959/66/pdfs/ukpga_1959 0066_en.pdf.

Parliament of the United Kingdom (2006), 'Racial and Religious Hatred Act 2006 (c. 1)'. http://www.legislation.gov.uk/ukpga/2006/1/contents.

Phelps-Roper v Strickland, United States Court of Appeals, Sixth Circuit, Aug 22, 2008539 F.3d 356 (6th Cir. 2008).

Post, R. (1991). 'Racist Speech, Democracy, and the First Amendment'. *William and Mary Law Review* 32: 267–327.

Post, R. (2007). 'Religion and Freedom of Speech: Portraits of Muhammad'. *Constellations* 14 (1): 72–90.

Post, R. (2011). 'Participatory Democracy and Free Speech'. *Virginia Law Review* 97(3): 477–89.

Post, R. (2017a). 'Legitimacy and Hate Speech', *Constitutional Commentary* 32(3): 651–9.

Post, R. (2017b). 'There Is No 1st Amendment Right to Speak on a College Campus'. *Vox*, 31 December. https://www.vox.com/the-big-idea/2017/10/25/16526442/first-amendment-college-campuses-milo-spencer-protests.

R v Butler [1992] 1 S.C.R. 452.

R v Lemon; R v Gay News Ltd [1979] 1 All ER 898.

R v Zundel [1992] 2 S.C.R. 731.

Rassinier, P. (1975). *The Drama of the European Jews*, translated by M. Hardesty (Silver Spring, MD: Steppingstones Publications).

Rawls, John. 2005. *Political Liberalism*, expanded edn (New York: Columbia University Press).

Raz, Joseph 1986. *The Morality of Freedom* (Oxford: Clarendon).

Reid, A. (2020). 'Does Regulating Hate Speech Undermine

Democratic Legitimacy? A Cautious "No"'. *Res Publica* 26(2): 181–99.
Riley, J. (2005). 'J. S. Mill's Doctrine of Freedom of Expression'. *Utilitas* 17(2): 147–79.
Rini, R. (2017). 'Fake News and Partisan Epistemology'. *Kennedy Institute of Ethics Journal* 27(2): 43–64.
Ross v New Brunswick School District No 15 [1996] 1 S.C.R. 825.
Rostbøll, C. F. (2009). 'Autonomy, Respect, and Arrogance in the Danish Cartoon Controversy'. *Political Theory* 37(5): 623–48.
Roth v United States, 354 US 476 (1957).
Ruddick, S. (1975). 'Better Sex', in R. Baker and F. Elliston (eds), *Philosophy and Sex* (Buffalo, NY: Prometheus Books), pp. 83–104.
Rushdie, S. (1988). *The Satanic Verses* (New York: Viking).
Sandel, M. (1984). 'Morality and the Liberal Ideal'. *New Republic* 190: 15–17.
Scanlon, T. M. (1972). 'A Theory of Freedom of Expression'. *Philosophy & Public Affairs* 1(2): 204–26.
Scanlon, T. M. (1979). 'Freedom of Expression and Categories of Expression'. *University of Pittsburgh Law Review* 40(4): 519–50.
Schauer, F. (1982). *Free Speech: A Philosophical Enquiry* (Cambridge: Cambridge University Press).
Schauer, F. (2012). 'Social Epistemology, Holocaust Denial, and the Post-Millian Calculus', in M. Herz and P. Molnar (eds), *The Content and Context of Hate Speech: Rethinking Regulation and Responses* (Cambridge: Cambridge University Press), pp. 129–44.
Schenck v United States, 249 US 47 (1919).
Seglow, J. (2016). 'Hate Speech, Dignity and Self-Respect'. *Ethical Theory and Moral Practice* 19(5): 1103–16.
Setälä, M. and G. Smith (2018). 'Mini-Publics and Deliberative Democracy', in A. Bächtiger, J. D. Dryzek, J. Mansbridge and M. E. Warren (eds), *The Oxford Handbook of Deliberative Democracy* (Oxford: Oxford University Press), pp. 300–14.
Sher, G. (2020) 'Taking Offense'. *Journal of Political Philosophy* 28(3): 332–42.
Shiffrin, S. V. (2011). 'A Thinker-Based Approach to Free Speech'. *Constitutional Commentary* 27 (2): 283–307.
Shiffrin, S. V. (2014). *Speech Matters: On Lying, Morality, and the Law* (Princeton, NJ: Princeton University Press).
Shoemaker, D. W. (2000). '"Dirty Words" and the Offense Principle'. *Law and Philosophy* 19(5): 545–84.
Simpson, R. (2013). 'Dignity, Harm, and Hate Speech'. *Law and Philosophy* 32(6): 701–28.

Simpson, R. (2018). 'Regulating Offense, Nurturing Offense'. *Politics, Philosophy and Economics* 17(3): 235–56.

Simpson, R. (2020). 'The Relation between Academic Freedom and Free Speech'. *Ethics* 130(3): 287–319.

Simpson, R. and A. Srinivasan (2018). 'No Platforming', in Jennifer Lackey (ed.), *Academic Freedom* (Oxford: Oxford University Press), pp. 186–209.

Snyder v Phelps, 562 US 443 (2011).

Stark, C. (1997). 'Is Pornography an Action? The Causal vs the Conceptual View of Pornography's Harm'. *Social Theory and Practice* 23(2): 277–306.

Strikwerda, L. (2017). 'Legal and Moral Implications of Child Sex Robots', in J. Danaher and N. McArthur (eds), *Robot Sex: Social and Ethical Implications* (Cambridge, MA: MIT Press), pp. 133–52.

Strossen, N. (2018). *Hate: Why We Should Resist It with Free Speech, Not Censorship* (Oxford: Oxford University Press).

Sunstein, C. (1993). *Democracy and the Problem of Free Speech* (New York: Free Press).

Sunstein, C. (2007). *Republic.com 2.0* (Princeton, NJ: Princeton University Press).

Teachout, P. (2006). 'Making "Holocaust Denial" a Crime: Reflections on European Anti-Negationist Laws from the Perspective of US Constitutional Experience'. *Vermont Law Review* 30(3): 655–92.

Ten, C. L. (1980). *Mill on Liberty* (Oxford: Clarendon).

Titley, G. (2020). *Is Free Speech Racist?* (Cambridge: Polity).

Turley v ISG Lackawanna, Inc., No. 13-561 (2d Cir. 2014).

United Nations (1969). *International Convention on the Elimination of All Forms of Racial Discrimination (ICERD)*. https://www.refworld.org/docid/3ae6b3940.html.

Virginia v Black, 538 US 343 (2003).

Waldron, J. (1987). 'Mill and the Value of Moral Distress'. *Political Studies* 35(3): 410–23.

Waldron, J. (2012). *The Harm in Hate Speech* (Cambridge, MA: Harvard University Press).

Waldron, J. (2017). 'The Conditions of Legitimacy: A Response to James Weinstein'. *Constitutional Commentary* 32(3): 697–714.

Warburton, N. (2009). *Free Speech: A Very Short Introduction* (Oxford: Oxford University Press).

Warren, M. E. and H. Pearse (eds) (2008). *Designing Deliberative Democracy: The British Columbia Citizens' Assembly* (Cambridge: Cambridge University Press).

Watson, L. (2010). 'Pornography'. *Philosophy Compass* 5(7): 535–50.

Weinstein, J. (2001). 'Hate Speech, Viewpoint Neutrality, and the American Concept of Democracy', in T. Hensley (ed.), *The Boundaries of Freedom of Expression and Order in American Democracy* (Kent, OH: Kent State University Press), pp. 146–69.

Weinstein, J. (2011). 'Participatory Democracy as the Central Value of American Free Speech Doctrine'. *Virginia Law Review* 97(3): 491–514.

Weinstein, J. (2017). 'Hate Speech Bans, Democracy and Political Legitimacy'. *Constitutional Commentary* 32(3): 527–83.

Wendell, S. (1983). 'Pornography and Freedom of Expression', in D. Copp and S. Wendell (eds), *Pornography and Censorship* (Buffalo, NY: Prometheus), pp. 167–83.

West, C. (2018). 'Pornography and Censorship', in E. N. Zalta (ed.), *The Stanford Encyclopedia of Philosophy*. https://plato. stanford.edu/archives/fall2018/entries/pornography-censorship.

Williams, B. (ed.) (2015). *Obscenity and Film Censorship: An Abridgement of the Williams Report* (Cambridge: Cambridge University Press).

Wright, P. J., R. S. Tokunaga and A. Kraus (2016). 'A Meta-Analysis of Pornography Consumption and Actual Acts of Sexual Aggression in General Population Studies'. *Journal of Communication* 66(1): 183–205.

Index